# Eugenio Balzan

1874-1953
A Biography

Renata Broggini

# Eugenio Balzan
1874-1953
A Biography

**EDITORE ULRICO HOEPLI MILANO**

Copyright © Ulrico Hoepli Editore S.p.A. 2007
via Hoepli 5, 20121 Milano (Italy)
tel. +39 02 864871 – fax +39 02 8052886
e-mail hoepli@hoepli.it

**www.hoepli.it**

All rights reserved in accordance with the law
and all international agreements

**ISBN 978-88-203-3948-7**

Reprint:
4  3  2  1  0          2007   2008   2009   2010   2011

Condensation of:
*Eugenio Balzan 1874-1953. Una vita per il "Corriere", un progetto per l'umanità*
Copyright © 2001 by RCS Libri S.p.A., Milano

Translation by Clarice Zdanski

Composition by Thèsis S.r.l., Firenze-Milano

Cover by MN&CG S.r.l., Milano

Printed by Legoprint S.p.A., Lavis (Trento)

Printed in Italy

# Contents

*Preface by Bruno Bottai*     7

*A Note on the Sources*     11

1. At *Corriere della Sera*     15

2. Balzan's Roots     37

3. Life in Milan     49

4. Mussolini Arrives on the Scene     59

5. Life in Switzerland     73

6. The Project     85

7. The Painting Collection     97

**Appendices**

Chronology     103

Biographical Sketches     109

# Preface

The Balzan Foundation is well known for the prestigious and generous prizes that it awards each year to members of the world of culture, to distinguished scholars in the fields of humanities or of scientific research and to individuals or institutions engaged in meritorious humanitarian initiatives of peace and brotherhood among peoples.

In the following pages, Renata Broggini traces Balzan's origins, from his birth in Badia Polesine in 1874, to his youth, his family's financial difficulties, his unhappy marriage, the birth of his daughter Lina, his first steps in journalism at *L'Arena* of Verona, and then the extraordinary adventure of being hired in Milan, at only 23 years of age, at *Corriere della Sera*. We can also read about his rapid success in the great Milanese newspaper. From proof-reader, he became a member of the editorial staff, then a successful roving correspondent, with important overseas assignments, and finally managing editor, whose authority grew continuously and who was always on the lookout for innovations that could increase the paper's circulation.

Despite his reserved nature, Balzan was soon well known not only among journalists, but also for his friendships with such famous figures as Arturo Toscanini, Luigi Barzini,

Giacomo Puccini, Gabriele D'Annunzio, Luigi Albertini, Curzio Malaparte and Arnoldo Mondadori. It was his involvement in such circles that inspired Balzan to start a painting collection with works from the main regional schools in Italy just after unification.

At the painful time when he was ousted from *Corriere* in the mid-thirties because of conflicts with the Fascist regime, Balzan did not hesitate to choose Switzerland as his refuge. In the Swiss Confederation, he spent those difficult years between Zurich and Lugano, until the tragic years of World War II. His life was no different from the lives of the many political refugees who were there, too. He knew many of them and often tried to help them. It was also in Switzerland – first in Zurich and then in Bellinzona – that Balzan exhibited his painting collection in 1943. He had it sent from Milan, which was under bombardment at the time.

To the close friends in whom he confided, Balzan often mentioned projects to which he wanted to leave his considerable estate. However, he never decided which ones to embark upon. When he died without making a will, his sole heir became his only daughter Lina, who had almost always lived far from him, but she nevertheless admired him. After making a number of bequests in her father's memory and many generous charitable donations, Lina Balzan decided to set up the E. Balzan International Foundation in 1957. It was to have humanitarian, social, scientific and artistic goals that were to be promoted by awarding generous prizes.

There is a special thread that runs through Eugenio Balzan's life between Switzerland and Italy, and it is echoed in the division of the Foundation into two headquarters, one in Milan, mainly dedicated to cultural activities and to the awarding of the prizes, and the twin office in Zurich, which has the task of administering the considerable estate of the Balzan inheritance. There is an analogy in the close relationship that unites Italy to the Swiss Confederation, which is based on the shared ideals of peace and co-operation. The Italian language of the Canton Ticino and part of the Grisons also nurtures this bond and makes it stronger.

The awarding of the Balzan Prizes takes place in a solemn ceremony, in alternate years in each country's capital, Rome or Berne, and the respective heads of State are present.

Ambassador BRUNO BOTTAI
Chairman of the Board
*International E. Balzan Foundation "Prize"*

# A Note on the Sources

While I was doing broader research on Italians in exile in Switzerland in the 1930s at the Federal Archive in Berne, I examined a dossier on Eugenio Balzan that concerned the period when, as an Italian living in Zurich, he was "under surveillance" by the Swiss Federal Police. I was given the task of going into greater depth on this still unknown matter when the International Balzan Foundation commissioned me to write a biography on the man for whom their institution was named and whose goals are represented in its rules and regulations.

Published in Italian with the title *Eugenio Balzan 1874-1953. Una vita per il "Corriere", un progetto per l'umanità* [*Eugenio Balzan 1874-1953. A Life for "Corriere", A Project for Mankind*] in 2001, it also required research work in the Veneto, in Badia Polesine, where the Balzan family was from, and in Verona, where other family members lived and where Eugenio Balzan's daughter Lina was born. Information on the family was taken from the posthumous book on Balzan's brother Luigi, *Viaggio di esplorazione nelle regioni centrali del Sud America* [*Exploration in the Central Regions of South America*, Milan, Treves (1931), now *Des Andes à l'Amazonie 1891-1893*, ed. Alain Gioda and Jean-Claude Roux, Paris, Ginkgo (2007)], in particular, the comments of the editor, Arnaldo Fraccaroli, a collegue of Eugenio Balzan. Other information of a personal nature and a brief autobiographical note by Balzan on his adolescence were traced through the letters of correspondents and photographs in the Archives of the International Balzan Foundation in Milan.

A fundamental source on the years he worked for *Corriere* and on his relationships – and not just business – with the Milanese milieu of the time is the historical archive of *Corriere della Sera* in Milan. Other useful publications are the memoirs of Alberto Albertini, *Vita di Luigi Albertini* (1945); the monograph *Corriere della Sera (1919-1943)* edited by Piero Melograni (1965); the biography *Albertini* by Ottavio Barié (1972); the history of the newspaper *Storia del "Corriere della Sera"* by Glauco Licata (1976); and the reconstructions and memoirs by Gaeano Afeltra, *Corriere primo amore* [*Corriere First Love* (1984)], by Luigi Barzini Jr., *Barzini Senior, Barzini Junior, Barzini Ludina* (1986) and by Paolo Murialdi, *Storia del giornalismo italiano* [*The History of Italian Journalism* (2000)].

At the Central State Archives and the historical-diplomatic Archives of the Ministry for Foreign Affairs in Rome, I traced documents that enabled me to carry out crosschecks on political events of the 1920s and '30s that were only hinted at in various works on the Fascist period, like Attilio Tamaro's *Venti anni di storia* [*Twenty Years of History* (1948)]; Giorgio Pini–Duilio Susmel's, *Mussolini l'uomo e l'opera [Mussolini: the Man and His Work* (1957)]; Renzo De Felice's *Mussolini il fascista. La conquista del potere 1921-1925* [*Mussolini The Fascist. The Conquest of Power 1921-1925* (1966)] and *La stampa italiana nell'età fascista* [*The Anti-Fascist Press in Italy in the Fascist Period* (1980)] by Nicola Tranfaglia, Paolo Murialdi and Massimo Legnani.

In order to reconstruct the milieu in Milan at the beginning of the twentieth century, with its leading figures who were also

*A Note on the Sources*

Balzan's friends, I read newspapers from the period in question, inlcuding *Corriere*, and *Storia illustrata di Milano, vol. V – Milano moderna* [*An Illustrated History of Milan, vol. V – Modern Milan*], ed. Franco Della Peruta (1993); Harvey Sachs, *Toscanini. Eine Biographie* [*Toscanini. A Biography* (1978)] and Piero Melograni *Toscanini* (2007).

For the "Swiss" years, I went to the State Archives in Bellinzona, in particular, the files *Italians Interned in Switzerland 1943-1945*, with notes on politicians and journalist colleagues, many of whom were Balzan's interlocutors. I also used this material in *Terra d'asilo. I rifugiati italiani in Svizzera 1943-1945* (1993), *La frontiera della speranza. Ebrei dall'Italia verso la Svizzera 1943-1945* (1998) [published in translation as *Frontier of Hope. Jews from Italy Seek Refuge in Switzerland, 1943-1945* (2003)].

My ideas for the study of Balzan's picture collection came from the Swiss catalogue *Italienische Malerei des XIX. Jahrhunderts. Ausstellung im Kunsthaus* [*Nineteenth Century Italian Painting. An Exhibit at the Kunsthaus*], ed. Giuseppe Delogu (1944); Filippo Sacchi, *Diario 1943-1944. Un fuoruscito a Locarno* [*Diary 1943-1944: An Exile in Locarno*], which I edited (1987), and the recent exhibit catalogue by Giovanna Ginex, with my contributions, *Storia di una collezione d'arte tra Ottocento e Novecento. La raccolta di Eugenio Balzan* (2006), published in English as *The History of an Art Collection. 19th and 20th Century Paintings Collected by Eugenio Balzan* (2006).

CHAPTER ONE

## At *Corriere della Sera*

In its one hundred thirty years of activity, *Corriere della Sera*, one of Italy's most widely circulated and authoritative newspapers, has launched the careers of many of the most famous journalists in Italy. But the origins of the success of this Milan-based paper – as with any business firm – can also be sought in the less visible sector of executive officers, writers, reporters, messenger boys or typographers, about whom little is known. Eugenio Balzan is one of these.

Among the figures who worked at *Corriere della Sera*, he towers over the rest not only because of his stature and formidable countenance, but also for the thirty years he acted as managing director of the paper (1903-1933) – "the truest, most authentic symbol of a way of thinking and code of behaviour that became a standard for the company", as he was remembered in an article in *Corriere* written on the occasion of his death, when some still remembered his 'legendary' administration.

Balzan's role was acknowledged by someone who had been at the highest ranks of the newspaper in the 1920s, co-owner and editor Alberto Albertini, in his biography on his brother Luigi Albertini, who had been dismissed in 1925 as a result of the imposition of Fascism. The biography came out in Rome in April 1945 while the purges were in progress and officials of the Fascist regime and their profiteering were being exposed. In reconstructing the manoeuvrings behind their expulsion from *Corriere*, Alberto emphasized that Balzan – who had been living in Switzerland since 1933, and therefore at the time Albertini was writing his work – was famous for his role as "lieutenant" in the management of the daily paper:

> He always showed a keen interest in the editorial part, but my brother was steadfast in keeping the powers of his two lieutenants separate. I don't think Balzan willingly accepted this delimitation, and in his heart of hearts, he longed to extend his field of authority to policy-making and editing. Nonetheless, we were on the best of terms until the crisis that caused our exit from the *Corriere* scene.

Despite his important position at the helm of *Corriere* for over thirty years, Balzan was almost forgotten because he had left Italy at a time when freedom of speech in the country was most seriously threatened by the Fascist regime. His absence during this crucial phase might seem ambiguous to many in the world of journalism. The impression that Balzan already belonged to a far-away period as early as in 1945, twelve years after his self-imposed exile, is confirmed by the silence that surrounded his last years. People started talking about him again as a leading figure in the history of the paper in 1953, when he died unexpectedly on 15 July in Lugano. In an unsigned article, *Corriere* remembered the managing director Balzan among "the most prized craftsmen of the nobility of Italian journalism, a teacher and an example of great dignity and inspiring activity."

"If Italian journalism owes him such recognition," concluded the writer of the article, "this word ought to be changed into recognition for the old *Corriere della Sera*, because in it and for it, his career and inspiration were fulfilled." In the same year, in a history of the twenty years of Fascism, former Minister Plenipotentiary of Italy in Switzerland (1935-1943) Attilio Tamaro acknowledged Balzan's exceptional influence as "the real power behind the creation of the Milanese newspaper":

> A great mind, ingenious organizer and untiring worker, Balzan gave the journal its wide circulation and developed its advertising, thus creating the industrial power the paper represented. He also chose many excellent collaborators and had the best editorial ideas. The paper owes its fortune much more to the highly organized work of penetration that he knew how to carry out like no other journalist in Italy than to the Albertinis' dry articles.

Then his figure faded until 1956, when the International Balzan Foundation was instituted in Lugano, through the wishes of Balzan's daughter Angela Lina, who used the considerable fortunes she had inherited for the plan that her father had referred to on various occasions: "great social and humanitarian work, of long and possibly perpetual duration." The Foundation reconfirmed Balzan's fame for generosity, but at the same time it ended up obscuring Balzan's role as journalist-entrepreneur by identifying him with the philanthropic initiative linked to his name. Luigi Barzini, Jr., son of one of *Corriere*'s greatest journalists and himself a journalist of note, wrote ironically: "Eugenio Balzan? For most people Balzan is only a name that is in circulation like an old, prize-winning liquor factory – the name of the very rich foundation that gives out fabulous prizes to well-deserving people."

Later, the first studies on journalism under the Fascists by Piero Melograni and Paolo Murialdi appeared (1980). They confirmed not only Balzan's influence on the leadership of the newspaper, but also his role in management when the ownership of *Corriere* was passed from the Albertini family to the Crespi family, as well as his importance in areas that lay outside the scope of the editorial staff: in other words, Balzan is an *éminence grise* to rediscover. Mario Mapelli, one of Balzan's most loyal secretaries, had already felt strongly about a "duty to remember the figure of Balzan." The Accademia dei Concordi of Rovigo, a cultural institution for which Balzan was benefactor, industrial associations in the Veneto and other institutions commemorated him in 1989 as the "true *homo faber*" of culture and business.

But there were still many mysteries to solve: why did he stay on at the *Corriere* headquarters in Via Solferino in Milan for eight years after the Albertini family had left and in a climate that was increasingly hostile to his administration? What drove him to leave *Corriere*? What were his relationships with the Fascists really like? How did he make his fortune? These are the tangled issues that must be confronted in reconstructing his biography for the International Balzan Foundation.

Founded in 1876 by Eugenio Torelli-Viollier from Naples, and bought out in 1898 by the Albertini brothers Luigi and Alberto, *Corriere della Sera* was an institution in the Lombard capital. In Milan – which counted 300,000 inhabitants at the time – eight newspapers of various political stances were published. It was not a matter of chance that this city, a leader in every sector, and especially in the humanities and sciences, had a rate of illiteracy far below the national average when the 1871 census was taken: 45% as opposed to 68%. This also explains the origins of the success of its many editorial firms.

In particular, *Corriere* jumped from 3,200 initial copies to 85,000 in 1896, and then to the spectacular printings of the Albertini-Balzan period: around 150,000 in 1906, which almost doubled in 1911, then 350,000 in 1918, and over 600,000 in 1920. During the First World War, as many as one million copies were printed due to its high-quality stories, efficiency and top-notch collaborators; circulation then levelled off to become stable at 800,000 copies daily. This success depended on the Albertini ownership, which transformed the newspaper into the semi-official mouthpiece – if not the spokesman – of government milieus. It also depended on Balzan, who set up and dealt with the administrative apparatus: advertising, editorial initiatives, distribution, labour disputes, supplies and personnel.

Balzan arrived at what would become the "Battleship *Corriere*" in the autumn of 1897, after a turbulent youth and some experience at *L'Arena*, which was the main daily newspaper of Verona at the time. Headed by one of the best journalists of the era, Giovanni Antonio Aymo, who was also owner, *L'Arena* printed 11,000 copies and was anything but provincial. From 1885-1895, the successful Italian writer Emilio Salgàri, best known for exotic adventure stories like *The Tiger of Malaysia* and *The Black Corsair* was employed as a sort of jack-of-all-trades reporter. The paper was a breeding ground for promising young writers.

Balzan's brief experience at the top-notch school of *L'Arena* gave him the rudiments of his trade and convinced him that he had found his calling: "I have felt an irresistible attraction to journalism," he stated, "over the past several years – years lived more seriously than I should have at my youthful age – I have dreamed of becoming a journalist." Called back to the land office in Verona, and forced to leave *L'Arena*, it seemed as though his dream had vanished. But he did not give up. When his job took him to Milan, he went to see another native of his hometown Badia, Adolfo Rossi, then editor-in-chief at *Corriere della Sera*, and asked about a job at the paper.

Called in to substitute a proof-reader, Balzan started work on 12 September 1897 at the daily paper, one of the most important in Italy, thus reaching his ideal. The *Corriere* staff included various journalists from the Veneto region in managerial positions, and these staff members supported him because of their common homeland. Moreover, Torelli-Viollier liked him and thought highly of him. After only three months, on 1 December, Balzan was promoted to editor. His career then took the fast track because of the serious social and political tensions in Milan at the turn of the century. In the spring of 1898, the high cost of bread caused protests in the squares, and the people constructed barricades as they had done in 1848, during the uprisings against the Austrians. Government repression in Rome, the work of General Bava-Beccaris, caused many deaths and the city was in a state of siege. *Corriere* refused to support the government's hard line, but some of the stockholders did – mainly to obtain the majority in controlling the paper – and thus undermine the director. On 10 June 1898, Torelli-Viollier stepped down, and the newspaper went to the Albertini brothers. Balzan kept his place in the family of *Corriere della Sera*, where he made a good impression because of his resourcefulness, hard work and his stories – two scoops in particular – that caused a sensation on a national level.

The first scoop involved the Italian Socialist Party, which held its general assembly 'behind closed doors' in Milan in January 1901. On this occasion, an inside dispute between two national leaders, Filippo Turati and Costantino Lazzari was the issue. Despite all of the party's precautions to keep journalists out, *Corriere* managed to publish highly detailed reports on the agitated discussions every morning. The newspaper managed this because Balzan hid under the stage of the theatre where the congress was held, and stayed there on into the night. He could recognize the various speakers by their voices, and took notes later by candlelight.

Turati came out as the winner of the dispute, but perhaps the greatest success went to *Corriere*. It was a great personal success for Balzan, too, who showed as much tenacity when he maintained a state of alert day and night in that same January of 1901, ever ready to be the first to accurately inform the public on the death of the famous musician Giuseppe Verdi, who was in his nineties by then, and ailing. The *maestro* was famous because his works made explicit references to Italy's independence from Austrian domination. In fact, cries of "Viva Verdi!" were a sort of acronym for cries of long-live-the-king, "*Viva Vittorio Emanuele Re D'Italia*", in support of Vittorio Emanuele II of Savoy to reunite all states and peoples of Italy under his sceptre. Verdi's death caused a great stir, as he was deeply loved, and performances of his world famous operas like *Aida*, *Nabucco* and *Il Trovatore* were successes first at Milan's La Scala and soon thereafter in the greatest opera houses throughout the world.

From the time that Verdi had had the stroke that was to be his fatal demise, Balzan's reporting was so punctual and detailed that the reader felt as if he were actually at the maestro's bedside. And along with the information regarding Verdi's health, Balzan included details about his life and work, thus also giving a comprehensive biography of the famous opera composer.

These successful stories put him in a positive light for the new director, Luigi Albertini, who then sent Balzan on a long travel stint, not only throughout Italy but also abroad. He was given important assignments, and his name began to appear on the front page next to Luigi Barzini, Sr.'s. Barzini, who had achieved his fame through his reporting from China on the Boxer Rebellion, was *Corriere*'s most widely read reporter.

Balzan earned his promotion as reporter with a difficult story that the paper wanted to publish in order to force the government to take action on a situation that had been dragging on for years: the condition of emigrants in an era when thousands of Italians were forced to look for work abroad

– especially overseas – because in Italy, people were living on the verge of starvation. In charge of a touchy story, the young Balzan managed to get readers involved, appreciate his writing and champion *Corriere*'s cause. In a few months, he had not only made a name for himself, but had also acquired fame.

It was not the first time that the Milanese newspaper had taken an interest in emigration, which, after its beginnings in the mid-nineteenth century, was at its peak from 1900 to 1920. A radical member of Parliament had re-opened this painful chapter, demanding that the "senseless adventurousness" that was sapping the life out of Italy come to an end. In 1901, an unusual demographic phenomenon could be noted among emigrants to Canada. Emigration was apparently not a phenomenon that concerned masses where all ages and sexes are represented, but only healthy men between the ages of 18 and 40, and with money. So there was something strange about this wave of emigration, and *Corriere* sent Balzan to find out more about the "distressing conditions of our emigrants" in Canada. Why were so many Italians going "without women, or families, with a double saddlebag on their shoulders and a lot of money in their pockets?" - as depicted by the famous illustrator Achille Beltrame, on one of the covers for *Domenica del Corriere*, the newspaper's highly successful Sunday supplement.

As a special reporter, Balzan found a way to work his way into the ranks of the emigrants and write an investigative report that came out in ten articles signed "e.f.b." in *Corriere* between 5 May and 10 June 1901. In detailed travel reports that always made the front page and took up five columns, his articles exposed infractions in emigration and speculation on Italians by Swiss "employment agencies" with contacts in Naples and Canada. These agencies were supposed to find jobs in Canada for young Italian males with enough means to pay their overseas passage, but the sad truth was that they abandoned their 'recruits' abroad after taking all their money. Thus *Cor-*

*riere's* misgivings turned out to be well-founded, because between March and April, around 2,500 Italians disembarked in Canada, but two-thirds of them ended up in the United States after endless tribulation and "vile speculation". This came out in the very first correspondence Balzan sent during the trip that would take him and the emigrants from Switzerland to Liverpool in England, then by ship to Halifax in Canada, where, unsuspected by any of the voyagers, they ended up in Montreal, unprovided for and not knowing what to do – except head south and cross the border.

Balzan asked the government to stop other Italians from going to Canada, and pointed out that "we must create a government agency to protect, inform and get people started at jobs. An agency which is being talked about in the new law on emigration", because "we must get these poor people out of the hands of these vampires who are tearing them to pieces."

Two interpellations were presented in the House. Parliament member Vittorio Cottafavi acknowledged *Corriere*'s role in uncovering the scandal: "Finally, I insist that we provide for the protection of the name of Italy and the satisfaction of the families of the victims: and from this podium, I praise *Corriere della Sera* and the other newspapers which have followed the tracks, steadfastly and courageously showing us the underhanded dealing and exploitation that has been going on with our fellow countrymen."

There were also echoes in Switzerland, because it was from Chiasso that unscrupulous individuals were sending these emigrants off to fend for themselves. *Corriere del Ticino*, the most widely-circulated Swiss-Italian newspaper, called upon the Swiss Federal Council to take action against the agencies that were involved in this irregular emigration traffic. Balzan concluded the series with a piece on the arrival of the emigrants in the United States. Balzan's story led the government to confront the question in a more concrete way, while at the same time forcing

Italian delegations to intervene. He also brought success to the newspaper above and beyond the national level: *Corriere* had reached its goal in sending him to cover the story.

When he came back from overseas, Balzan had already obtained a position. The newspaper got him to conduct interviews with important people, and to do important investigations and other press campaigns that reflected the editorial line of *Corriere*. His articles always came out on the front page, and he wrote the Milanese column for other newspapers he corresponded for. His abilities earmarked him for a future career as manager.

And so he began to act as correspondent for papers outside Milan, like *Il Secolo XIX* of Genoa, Venice's *La Gazzetta di Venezia*, *Il Pungolo* of Naples and Sicily's *Il Giornale di Sicilia*, and foreign newspapers, like the *La Sentinella* of Chicago. A meticulous press review, the comparison of different versions, always confirming facts – these were the characteristics that made it possible to recognize Balzan's style even if he did not sign his articles. Whether writing about government matters or social events, he put his heart and soul into it, with concise, complete reporting that left no room for rebuttal.

Among important investigations that were assigned to Balzan, there was an international affair that threatened relations between Rome and Berne, the so-called Silvestrelli affair of 1902, a consequence of the trial of the Italian anarchist Gaetano Bresci, who, after his arrival from the United States, assassinated King Umberto I as retaliation for the deaths that had occurred during the revolt of 1898 in Milan. Although the European press condemned the episode, an anarchist newspaper from Geneva couched the episode in different terms, making a distinction between a bloody act of terrorism and a political attempt.

Thus the case caused a controversy about anarchists, who were tolerated in Switzerland, in a touchy period when there were constantly plots to overthrow the heads of state and gov-

## At Corriere della Sera

ernments in Europe. The Minister of Italy in Berne, Giulio Silvestrelli, objected to the Swiss government's toleration of the anarchist press, causing a misunderstanding and the breaking off of diplomatic relations. The Italian press gave a great deal of coverage to the dispute. *Corriere* gave the assignment to Balzan, whose correspondence from Berne – where he sought out the necessary contacts – showed his great skill in handling such a delicate matter with equanimity.

Thus, during those years as correspondent, Balzan also made himself known as a formidable, uncompromising organizer. He is described as "gruff, intractable, surly, very kind, and almost maniacal about a thousand little things, like all men who live alone." An "exquisite and almost feminine sensitivity that hides behind severe, almost surly appearances", as well as a "tenacious, inflexible nature: he would not accept compromises with work or with his conscience" are among the aspects of his personality mentioned by Luigi Barzini, Jr. Alberto Albertini wrote in his memoirs:

> He was cut out big and when I say this, I am not just thinking of his height or his broad chest, or his nervous wiriness, his hard, bony countenance, his conqueror's stride. Physically, with his cuirassier's stature and very masculine face, Balzan is an impressive man. Seeing him walking around with his head high and his great threatening strides, rending the air with his cane brandished in his enormous hand, he looks like someone going to battle, or someone who has to make the streets of the city his own. On his low forehead, furrowed above his light coloured eyes and his vigorous features, a hurricane is always stirring. If fury breaks out, he is a giant who springs to his feet, stretching out to the unfortunate one before him, making fists to thrash him, beating on the table as if to smash it to pieces, shout-

ing threats and reproaches, blaspheming the Mother of God. From him, there truly emanates a sense of raw material and brute force.

"You will go very far," Luigi Albertini told him, and Albertini understood human nature. In January 1903, he appointed Balzan managing director of the firm and in 1905 he nominated him arbitrator for disputes abroad. "Taxing work", noted Balzan in his summary *Cos'era amministrare il Corriere* [*What it was like to manage* Corriere], and in ten terse lines, he listed his responsibilities and the positions he had held in many years. One of his main priorities was to improve services to subscribers, newsstand distribution and advertising, which up to that time had been dealt with by an external agency, Haasenstein & Vogler, a firm managed by the Swiss Ercole Lanfranchi. With agencies throughout Italy, it was the sole authorized dealer. Prices for *Corriere della Sera* were fixed by contract until 1904. But with Albertini the direction had started to do business on equal terms, and Balzan's intervention can be detected in the notorious brusque tone of the writings. After conducting a survey on the efficiency of want ads, he got *Corriere* to start managing its own advertising, with great economic benefits because costs for bids were lowered, and so profits could be cashed in on.

Getting ads became so profitable that it was necessary to open booths in the Galleria Vittorio Emanuele downtown. Most of the advertising came out in periodicals that flanked the daily newspaper, like the Sunday publication *La Domenica del Corriere,* a leader because of its quality and colour printing since 1899; the more refined monthly literary supplement *La lettura* with writings by major contemporary authors (since 1901); *Il romanzo mensile* which printed a novel every month (since 1903) or the successful children's publication *Corriere dei Piccoli* (since 1908). With its humorous texts and colour illustrations, this magazine was an incentive for the family to read the newspaper together, and the regular features and characters in its stories were well-loved by all members of society.

The success of so many periodicals attracted advertisers, and the volume of business increased for two decades. Difficulties arose later, when competition from radio broadcasting started in 1924 and almost immediately caused a crisis. Balzan was sceptical about the relationship between newspapers and the radio, because the radio had the privilege of being able to broadcast news when newspapers were forced to be silent by the laws on Sunday's rest. The radio also gave space to newscasting and advertising, and aggravated the already destitute conditions newspapers were in. Balzan's point of view was always in the interests of the firm.

*Corriere*'s circulation was another thorny problem. Here, too, business as usual had its problems: there were few newsstands; newsagents wanted their cuts; means of communications were limited in an era when only the telephone and telegraph existed to cover long distances. But other problems were out of the ordinary: in an era when distribution depended on railway transport, holding up the departure of a train from a local hub could keep *Corriere* off the newsstands in entire regions, and thus let competitors get the edge. *Corriere*'s competitors used these tactics to keep the paper out of their territory. In the period after WWI, expansion policies included buying newspapers in order to eliminate competitors or reach a more widely varied public. This is what happened with the humoristic newspaper *Guerin Meschino,* which was bought out by *Corriere* in 1927 – another initiative on the part of Balzan.

Ever since the beginning of the 1920s, Balzan's main concern was the supply of raw materials, mainly paper. This was something that went beyond *Corriere*'s immediate concerns, as when he got the daily newspaper editors' union, which he was spokesman for, to vote on an agenda dealing with the conditions imposed upon newspapers by paper producers, whom he accused of having created a paper cartel. Amidst ups and downs, the matter went on for almost ten years between proposals for some degree of settlement and petitions to the Minister of Finances to abolish customs duty so that the quality of paper not available in Italy could be bought abroad. Finally, an agreement was reached at the end of 1921 in Rome through Balzan's mediation with newspaper labour union representatives and the Italian government.

As administrator, Balzan's chief concern was always the newspaper. It is true that he was no longer a reporter, but he still took his employees' interests to heart. But when it came to negotiations with trade unions, he had to make unpleasant decisions at times. He was inflexible when it came to workers' demands which he thought were unjustified, as Albertini noted, "In the times of strike-mania that paralysed the paper from time to time, Balzan got the idea to create a group of strike-breakers among our workers, ready to cross the picket line. It seemed impossible to get there, and even more so to get them to live in peace with the others, but Balzan went through his men one by one. It took months, but he managed."

Despite his rigour in running the business in the interest of its owners, Balzan was sensitive to the needs of his workers and was among the promoters of trade union benefits: compensation, bonuses, organization and time off. Moreover, as Chairman of the Italian Federation of Editors since 1921, he dedicated his efforts to the Class Contract, described as one of the best, and provided for a mutual company for *Corriere* employees. He took all of these matters very seriously, and the stress often took its toll on his health.

Balzan's responsibilities increased when he was nominated chief executive of the firm in 1918. In learning to cope with running the firm, he eventually became the *alter ego* to director/owner Luigi Albertini. The beginning of the 1920s, with scarcity of raw materials and inflation, added the post-war crisis to Balzan's problems in managing a firm of such a size, committed to maintaining its leading role through investment in machines and 'buying' prestigious reporters.

Besides taking care of personnel matters, as manager, he also had the task of recruiting new reporters from among the most famous – and hence the most demanding – journalists of the time and to find a balance between their demands and the interests of the firm. In policy-making, he usually opted for compromise solutions.

There were cases in which capable, esteemed reporters put his patience to the test, as in the case of the painter Massimo Campigli. Campigli's real name was Max Ihlenfeld, and he was from Berlin. Hired in 1913, he was a volunteer in WWI, and signed the stories he sent from the front "Campigli, born in Florence." Taken prisoner by the Austrians, he escaped and reached Moscow, sending stories on the odyssey of his return to *Corriere*, with first-hand news from Bolshevist Russia. Once back in Italy, Albertini sent him to Paris as correspondent, where 'Campigli' became so impassioned about art that he forgot about reporting because he was too busy painting. Balzan humoured him when it came time to quit his job as reporter by making arrangements for him not to lose benefits by leaving the firm with severance pay by 1926. Campigli became famous in Europe in the 1930s as a post-Cubist and Purist painter, and exhibited at the Biennale in Venice and Triennale in Milan.

There are also humorous accounts about how Balzan dealt with dubious receipts presented for reimbursement, as is the case with Guelfo Civinini, a colourful, travelling reporter whose habit of presenting 'imaginary' receipts is recalled by the renowned journalist Indro Montanelli:

> The most famous thing about him in the history of *Corriere* is the 'legal dispute' that he had with the unyielding, parsimonious Balzan (the one of the Prize) over bills that have always existed, ever since newspapers and reporters have had an opportunity to engage in a dispute. Civinini had two clashes with him. The first occurred when he expected to be reimbursed for losing at the gambling house in Montecarlo because, as he said, only at the roulette table – truly high class – was he able to get an interview with Bella Otero, the most beautiful of the *Belle Epoque* beauties, who would never let anyone interview her. Balzan did not budge on this point: at most, he said, he could reimburse a special envoy for losses at innocent card games like *briscola* or *scopone*. Balzan gave in, strangely enough, to another request for reimbursement, because it appealed to 'reasonable terms' for 'female' collaboration (to be understood in the broadest of senses). The receipts were to be put under the heading 'man is not made of wood', a wry twist on 'the flesh is weak' that sent all his colleagues at *Corriere* into raptures. Unfortunately, slightly later, Civinini, who was always hasty and careless about his receipts, presented one in which he was not made of wood for not one, but two times at the same sitting. Balzan added for the last time: 'nor is he made of iron', and refused to reimburse his reporter, and, amidst general consternation, then finally abolished the heading.

After the First World War, Balzan's responsibilities continued to increase when Luigi Albertini was nominated senator and went to Washington for a conference on the Far East in 1921-22. As he became more and more involved in the Italian political crisis, he left the direction of the newspaper to his brother Alberto until 1925. "It is difficult to separate the merits of one Albertini from the other", wrote Ambassador Sergio Romano in an article in *Corriere* (2001), "they both had the same fighting spirit, the same organizational spirit, the same civic pride."

The same can be said about Balzan, especially after the Albertini brothers had been forced to sell out. Balzan as manager was omnipotent, and made everything his business: foreign relations, the Rome office, employees, relations with colleagues and politicians. The following account of a meeting between renowed *Corriere* reporter Orio Vergani and Gabriele D'Annunzio, the poet of the Decadentism as well WWI fighter pilot, is from Curzio Malaparte, famous journalist and writer as well as an agent in the Allies' campaign in Italy in 1944, and one of the best known writers of the Fascist and post-WWII era. The story, issued in the magazine *Tempo*, caricatures Balzan's all-reaching power:

> Several years before the death of Gabriele D'Annunzio, Orio Vergani was summoned by Balzan, managing director of *Corriere della Sera*, and told: 'The Commander [i.e., D'Annunzio] telephoned me to tell me that he had something to say to the people of Italy, and that he would like one of our reporters to go to the Vittoriale immediately to take down his words. He mentioned your name to me, because he knows you already, and likes you. So leave at once for Gardone, where the Commander is impatiently waiting for you.' As he spoke, Balzan groomed his enormous, famous hands that were like half-kilo Florentine steaks. Vergani ran to the station and left. Gabriele D'Annunzio greeted him with his usual kindly cordiality. He had a weakness for Orio, whom he had not seen for years, and was amazed at

his extraordinary corpulence. 'You have come,' Gabriele told him, 'to resemble the *Hercules of Pratolino.*' D'Annunzio, on the contrary, had come to resemble an ivory statuette: he had become small, thin and smooth. His round, nude skull, with its withered skin marked by green veins, and his face full of wrinkles – baggy and sagging with his sharp, transparent nose and toothless mouth. His injured eye seemed to be white, still, watery; the good eye, by now without a brow and dim, moved slowly under a reddened lid. [ndt: D'Annunzio had lost sight in one of his eyes after a flying accident in WWI.] He had miniscule hands - like a doll's - two wax hands, arms, or rather, limbs, slender, emaciated, fragile and minute like two chicken bones. He was a very ancient old man - decrepit, gummy, toothless: the image of that horrid old age of which Gabriele was terrified, like the most horrible evil of man. 'How strong you are!' D'Annunzio exclaimed, looking at Vergani in awe and admiration. 'But I'm stronger than you are. If you want to try to wrestle with me, I'll pin you to the ground in just a few minutes.' And he added that, in order to be good at wrestling in ancient Greek and Roman times, it was necessary to know Greek and Latin syntax thoroughly. 'In fact,' he said, 'that is why when it comes to Greco-Roman wrestling, no one can beat me. Do you want to try?' And so he went on, stretching out his little chicken-bone arms, and wrapping them around the waist of Vergani's great body. D'Annunzio started to writhe about, to gasp, to mumble – trying to bend his Herculean adversary to the ground. But when Vergani felt the grip of those two limp, bony arms around his body, and when he saw that nude, yellow skull resting on his chest, he felt such great repulsion that he wanted to grab Gabriele by the neck, give him a big shove and send him flying against the wall of the Vittoriale. But

## At Corriere della Sera

all of a sudden a cloud opened in the sky, and Balzan appeared. Holding in his two enormous hands the front page of *Corriere della Sera*, Balzan showed him a great seven-columned headline: 'Gabriele D'Annunzio assassinated by our special envoy.' And with super-human force, Vergani held back.

As manager, Balzan truly made all of the decisions, and this is also because he was co-owner of a partnership share since 1925, when Benigno Crespi's sons Aldo, Mario and Vittorio Crespi took over. Benigno Crespi had died in 1910 and left everything to his sons: textile companies, farms, hydroelectrical plants, real estate firms and the partnership shares of *Corriere*. When the shares of the other partners were bought out in 1920, the Crespi, despite their 35 shares, were nevertheless on the sidelines with respect to Luigi Albertini, who only had 25, but, as senator, had had political clout: this is what caused the discord and intrigues to oust him. When the other partners were bought out, the Crespi became sole owners. One partnership remained for Balzan, who had contributed to managing the delicate transaction with the head of the Mussolini government.

Balzan's role as co-owner thrust him into the limelight, especially in various negotiations to eliminate rival newspapers and strengthen *Corriere*'s monopoly, even if he did not always agree with the directives of the new Fascist government, which had become a dictatorship by that time. Among the daily papers in Milan when Balzan was hired, the real enemy of *Corriere* was *Il Secolo*, the newspaper of the Republican, radical left. It had also become synonymous with wide circulation, so much so that when the inhabitants of Milan wanted a newspaper, they said: "give me a *secolo*." Balzan was very clever in using a play on words to express his aims in this respect. 'Secolo' means 'century' in Italian, and he made his message very clear in December 1899, when he turned newsvendors loose in the streets crying "the end of the century... the end of the century" ("la fine del secolo... la fine del secolo!"). Life has its quirks, and so it would be up to him to get rid of his 'rival' twenty-five years later, in the tangled web of private and executive policies in a regime that ruled through *diktat*. It was a bitter victory for the manager of *Corriere*, forced as he was to cope with compromises and pressures in a turbulent atmosphere, while a social class without scruples imposed itself on traditional values and even Fascism itself was rent through feuds between the *ras* and local potentates. The forced merger of *Il Secolo* and *Corriere* is the fruit of this complicated situation.

In 1926, one of the owners of *Il Secolo*, the well-known, powerful publisher Arnoldo Mondadori, took advantage of the political situation to try to get the upper hand on *Corriere*. But *Il Secolo* did not get off the ground, and Mondadori abandoned the initiative, leaving his other shareholder, Senatore Borletti, with a company full of debts. Borletti wanted to sell out, and so Mussolini forced the Crespi brothers to buy *Il Secolo*. A tangle of telegrams back and forth between Rome and Milan involving the Duce, the prefect and the owners characterizes the negotiations between the Crespi and Borletti. Balzan had eventually to make all of the decisions in defining the ticklish arrangements Rome imposed for the merger.

The *Il Secolo* affair is exemplary: Mussolini made a flailing newspaper part of *Corriere* and incorporated his "boys" in the editorial staff. Moreover, he directed part of his moderate readers towards *Il Secolo-Sera* – which was born of the merger. This was a clear move towards Fascistization that had not been taken when the Albertini family was forced out. At the end of the year, after a sudden, secret decision of the Great Fascist Council, Ugo Ojetti (who had been editor-in-chief of *Corriere* since March 1926) was replaced: the purgings demanded by

## At Corriere della Sera

Fascist party officials and *petits fonctionnaires* of the provinces had found more obstacles than they had bargained for at *Corriere*. Some of Balzan's appointments were defined as 'of the old Albertinian type', and Ojetti's style too 'cultural'. There was even word of conflicts between Ojetti and Balzan over certain hirings that had not been made.

Of course, the *Secolo* merger represents the height of Balzan's power. At the age of fifty, he dealt with great industrialists, leading figures in the world of politics and even with the head of the government himself, Benito Mussolini. He had come an extraordinarily long way for a tormented youth who had left the provinces of the Veneto.

CHAPTER TWO

# Balzan's Roots

Despite the fact that Balzan lived the most intense part of his life in Milan at the helm of *Corriere della Sera*, he came from another part of Italy, the Veneto, which shaped his character, and had important consequences for the humanitarian and philanthropic projects he undertook later in life.

Eugenio Francesco Balzan was born on 20 April 1874 in Badia Polesine, a town in the river plain where the Po and Adige rivers meet in the Veneto region, a little over 100 kilometres from Venice. In search of a more interesting cultural milieu, the family had moved there around the middle of the nineteenth century from the tiny town of Masi on the opposite bank of the Adige River. Badia's origins went all the way back to the ancient Roman agrarian system set up after the seventh century A.D. in Wangadicia, the name of the territory that reached from the Po-Adige alluvial plain all the way north to the area around Padua and Verona. In that strategic position, a monastery rose in the Middle Ages, and was expanded by continuous donations by Frankish and Lombard lords and by the Estense family. The monastery became the centre of the future town of Badia.

Located in a key point of the Adige Valley Centuriation, the village was re-fortified in the Middle Ages with towers – three of which appear on the town's coat of arms – and with moats that marked the city plan at that time, between the Adige River and the Adigetto Canal. A noted Badia inhabitant, Gian Girolamo Bronziero, physician and historiographer of the seventeenth century, wrote that the inhabitants had found safety, a healthy lifestyle and easy navigation there, as well as "a lookout corner, because it was where the two branches of the Adige come together." It became a city in 1817. When the Balzans moved there it was part of the Kingdom of Lombard-Veneto, instituted in 1815 and subject to the Austrian Empire. After 1859 the Austrian realm was reduced to the Veneto only, since Lombardy was lost and the border shifted to follow the course of the Mincio River.

Balzan came from a family of landowners with a strong sense of Italian Risorgimento values in a part of Italy that was still under Austrian domination. Eugenio's mother, Angela Lina Bonato, was from Padua; his father, Lorenzo, a property administrator by profession, was a striking individual, a very handsome man of athletic proportions and Herculean strength as well as a generous soul. Once a week, the poor could go to his house for a meal, and so many came that they filled the courtyard. There are many tales of his physical strength. One of the best goes like this: a haughty Austrian Hussar official liked to ride his horse into the main café in town and treat the Italian bar owner and customers with a patronizing air. One day Lorenzo Balzan decided he had had enough of seeing these people treated like slaves, and so he dragged both horse and rider into the street and knocked them down.

Lorenzo was a passionate patriot, and did nothing to hide his sentiments. He was even sent to prison on the accusation of belonging to the political association Giovine Italia and helping many of Badia's citizens to escape to the Piedmont, thus playing a part in the campaign to free the Veneto. He was arrested, but managed to be discharged. Patriotism ran in the family. Lorenzo's father Luigi had given hospitality to the poet and patriot Aleardo Aleardi, a leading figure of "rowdy anti-Austrian demonstrations" along with other students from Padua, and was a friend of fellow patriots from the Veneto Niccolò Tommaseo and Daniele Manin, key figures in the insurrections against Austrian domination. The Balzan home was steeped in Risorgimento values and the family was involved in the events that led up to the Italian Wars of Independence, the unification of Italy in 1861 and the separation of the Lombard-Veneto region from the Austrian Empire in 1866.

Lorenzo's sister, Luisa Balzan, was also involved in patriotic, anti-Austrian incidents. Every now and then she would cross the Po River with documents of great value to the Italian cause hidden in her dress. Over two hundred letters between this fascinating, graceful and intelligent aunt of Eugenio's and the poet Aleardi survive, documenting a friendship that lasted thirty years.

At this time, the Balzans, who were a family of well-to-do landowners, became interested in culture and travelled a great deal, thus showing their ambitions to vie with the nobility and the upper classes of the city. Eugenio's uncle Paolo Balzan, who had been mayor of Badia for twenty years as well as president of the beautiful little town theatre, had a strong interest in music and the arts. The little theatre was considered to be one of the most beautiful and elegant in Italy, and was even compared to Venice's Teatro Fenice.

Eugenio, too, had the same interests. He was exuberant, generous and proud. The friendships he kept were lasting, just as he held a grudge against those who initially rubbed him the wrong way. As far as relationships were concerned, honesty, rigour and excess are the story of his life. Fascinated by the world of art, he began collecting nineteenth century Italian paintings; he helped writers and playwrights; he held administrative positions at Milan's opera house La Scala; he presented the project to restore his hometown's "little Fenice" theatre (after the very famous one in Venice) at his own expense.

His brothers and sisters, Luigi, Paolo, Lavinia, Maria and Edvige, also had special talents. The first-born, Luigi, was an outstanding man, and is perhaps 'the famous Balzan' as far as Italians are concerned, since he was sited in the famous biographical dictionary Larousse. After his secondary school studies at the Foscarini Liceo in Venice, he took his university degree in natural sciences at Padua, then emigrated to Paraguay, where he taught in Asunción. In 1890, the Italian Geographical Society and the museum of natural history in Genoa sent him on a voyage of exploration in Chile, Peru and Bolivia, and his reports were published posthumously by Eugenio, since he died very young of malaria in Padua in 1893 at the age of 28. Recently, a French translation of his travel journals has been published.

Eugenio always "venerated" this brother, and had the occasion to show it later in life when he 'rediscovered' him as teacher and explorer in Bolivia and Paraguay. This came about thanks to a friend and colleague at *Corriere* who was also from Balzan's homeland. Arnaldo Fraccaroli, correspondent in South America in 1930, published an article in *Corriere della Sera* on Luigi Balzan's activity in Asunción.

The article was noticed by Badia municipal authorities, who were interested in this citizen who had brought the town prestige through his work in the sciences, and so they suggested publishing a collection of Luigi's writings and lectures. Eugenio was unable to follow up on the matter because when his brother had died he was far away from his family. Moreover, he had no documentation, so he sent his fellow townsmen to the Società Geografica Italiana in Rome, the organization that had sent Luigi on his voyage.

When Luigi's manuscript on his explorations, *Viaggio di esplorazione nelle regioni del Sud America*, was found, Balzan had it published. The city of Badia Polesine formed an honorary committee, and on 27 September 1931, the explorer was commemorated in a ceremony to place a stone plaque in the arcade of the town hall. The *Corriere* 'family' was present, inlcuding Aldo Borelli, the director, and different journalists who were friends of Eugenio's.

On that occasion, Balzan also set aside a considerable sum of money for a scholarship for Badia natives enrolled in biology and natural sciences at the university of Padua. In recognition of the occasion, the nearby city of Rovigo named a street after Luigi, as did Badia with its Riviera L. Balzan. The inauguration, which the town's citizens took to heart, was transformed by the authorities into a rally for the Fascist regime: vigorous support by the Duce's brother Arnaldo Mussolini, Fascist hobnobbing, the party song *Giovinezza*, pennants, black shirts, a speech by the podestà, a toast to the king, salutations to the Duce. While all this was going on, the authorities came forward to ask for part of the money for the Fascist youth organization, the Opera Nazionale Balilla. This ceremony, however, caused Balzan embarrassment and pain, as he was already on the outs with several of the Fascist *ras*.

The town hall records show a second, personal donation by Balzan to assist unemployed factory workers, needy individuals and families, and cultural and artistic initiatives by Badia citizens. The amounts were always in the millions, and connected to the memory of his brother or other family members who, after the loss of their property, could no longer regularly attend school nor invest in their inclinations for art and culture.

His sister Edvige, for example, showed talent for the theatre, and his other sister Maria was gifted at music, but they could not pursue their interests or develop their talents as they would have liked because of the hardships the family had to face when they moved to Padua in 1881 so that their children could go to school. It seems that the move may have also been caused by his father's gambling losses. Eugenio himself said that the family had lost everything because of his father's extravagant lifestyle: "He was a man who loved life. He drove around in a carriage and gave credit to everyone". In Badia, it was easy to dissipate all of the family's land possessions in the course of two or three decades, especially since social conditions had changed and higher taxes had been levied by the unified Italian government.

In particular, there were special taxes related to the flood of 1882 - less than an year after the Balzans' arrival in Padua, in fact, the Adige River broke its banks with a fury, flooding the countryside, and even threatening Padua and Verona. Nature had gone berserk. In a few days the situation had become tragic, and Masi was severely damaged. The Balzan family was in "dire straits" because their earnings from their agricultural holdings were lost, and their "sad estate" was worsened when they all had to go to work. Lorenzo, the father, found work in Venice, while Luigi attended university, Paolo went to technical school and Eugenio was in compulsory school. When Lorenzo secured a position as general overseer at Valli Mocenighe in the Veneto region, the family moved there and Eugenio found work decorating pottery.

The family returned to Padua in 1888, but even harder times were in store for them. Lorenzo could not find a job, and so began a life of hardship and poverty. Eugenio's brother Luigi was far away in South America. His other brother Paolo was a volunteer in the artillery, and after three years of moving around between Caserta, Venice and Treviso, tried to kill himself because of debts he could not pay off. After he got better, he was transferred to Padua and then discharged.

Eugenio had the opportunity to make a change for the better in his life when his aunt Luisa – the poet Aleardi's muse

– invited him to move to Verona, where he would remain until 1897 amidst continual comings and goings: "in the meantime, my family had fallen into a miserable state, and when I went to visit them, I took money and trunks full of food." In the well-to-do city of Verona, with its flourishing social life, he experienced moments of serenity after a difficult childhood that would leave its mark for the rest of his life.

The months went by in Verona, and his carefree life with his aunt soon made him a restless adolescent with a will to find out what life was really all about. Driven by idleness to the "places of perdition" in Verona and Padua, he got a taste of that hedonistic, scintillating world that other Balzans before him had known: "my trips to Venice and Padua became more and more frequent, and I frantically began to squeeze loads of money out of my poor aunt Luisa." He did, however, have more serious plans: "I wanted to start studying painting again, but at that time, at the end of the 90s, I also wanted to embark on a military career, and so I began to study in September of 1890." He thus surrounded himself with private tutors in order to get ready for the necessary exams.

His aunt Luisa took it upon herself to support him while he was enrolled at the academy in Modena. But then, when he least expected it, "I saw Itala one day in Piazza delle Erbe while I was buying fruit, and I fell in love with her." Meanwhile, in order to be accepted at the academy, he had to take exams at the recruiting centre in Padua, but in January of 1892, he suddenly found that he had responsibilities and hardships to face: Itala Adami was pregnant, his father was opposed to a shotgun wedding and his aunt had died. He and Itala had a church – but not a civil – ceremony. He had to make arrangements for a family and desperately began looking for a job, which he found in a firm in Milan.

On 17 May 1892, his daughter Angela Luigia Maria – Lina for short – was born in Verona. Eugenio wrote: "I could not stand being in Milan any longer and longed to return to my family, who were still with my parents. So I asked for a month's leave of absence, which was not granted, and so I resigned." When he returned, however, life at home started to become "an inferno of mutual insults", and so he went to live with his brother Paolo in Noventa Paduana, where he stayed for a few months, taking care of his uncle and his mother. But Paolo died at the age of twenty-four in November. Eugenio briefly went back to his wife, then tried again for a military job with the Carabinieri police force, but did not succeed because by that time, he had a family.

He then tried to enlist in the Savoy Cavalry regiment, and was accepted. Then more high living and another infatuation brought on "a new illness [venereal disease] that lasted until October of the same year". In September 1893 he received the unexpected news of the death of his brother Luigi, which touched him deeply. When Eugenio enlisted for the draft, he was assigned to "Category III" because he was the "only son of a living father" which meant that he would probably be discharged. He then got a job in the cadastre in the city of Verona, where he worked for a few years.

Perhaps the death of the brother he had so greatly admired inspired him to make an effort to get his qualifications and find a decent job. He applied to take the exams for admission to the course in surveying at the technical institute in Mantua, and succeeded with the help of his father's friends and former Badia natives in high places. By 1896, he had reached a balance in his professional life. In Mantua he attended night school for town clerks, passed, and took his exams in surveying after resigning from the cadastre. However, his family life took a turn for the worse: his father had to go into a rest home run by charity, his sister Lavinia's health worsened and she died just after turning twenty-five. Eugenio found out about it when he was in Mantua, away from home, and not among his loved ones. Another tragedy occurred in 1898 with the death of his father, but Eugenio had at least found a direction in life by that time.

He took exams in topography and agriculture in Turin, and then took up his job again at the cadastre in Verona. During this period records show that he travelled throughout the Veneto region while working for a surveying firm. It was then that he put an advertisement in *Corriere della Sera*: "Young surveyor, twenty-three years old, of a very distinguished family, with experience in Italian and French correspondence, neat handwriting, seeks employment in business, as a land agent or as a secretary for a family. Excellent qualifications and references. Write to 'GB posta Verona'." It did not appear that the advertisement had any results, which is a sign that surveying was not Balzan's true calling. In fact, he began to write stories for Verona's newspaper *L'Arena*, where he learned the trade and received his membership card from the editor-in-chief of that rigorous "school of journalism" headed by Giovanni Antonio Aymo:

> Dear Balzan. I enclose your membership card. In asking me to hand it over to you, the Editor is breaking with the traditions of this newspaper, because he has exonerated you from the long trial period which is customary for all newly hired writers. Exempting you from this practise is not just a sign of the esteem that the newspaper has for you, but above all, it is a sign of the trust it has in you. You must be diligent and careful – especially in reporting the news. Published news must be the truth. Establish relations with the sources directly. And in questionable cases (such as crime stories) do not forget police headquarters and the clerks of court. Make sure your stories are packed with information, and choose your words well so as to avoid clichés. In general, keep to

the facts and do not make asides. Remember that your readers know how to think for themselves. You must instil in them the conviction that when they read reports from Vicenza, they are 1) sure that they are reading the truth, and 2) not wasting time.

When his review of a play performed at the theatre in Vicenza was well-received, Balzan was convinced that he had chosen the right way in life. After being summoned to Verona, he was driven to aim for a career in journalism, and so he went to *Corriere della Sera* in Milan. His letters to and from his friends in the Veneto reveal his ambitious plans. "I see you are looking on high, and not in a mystical sense," said one of his colleagues at the Verona paper.

When he was finally hired at *Corriere della Sera* and settled in Milan, he was joined by five women in 1898 – his mother, sisters, wife and daughter – a demanding family group that he, a young man only in his twenties, had to take care of. He worked very hard, mainly to keep expenses under control. His marriage was in a shambles, but he never lost touch with his wife, until the official annulment of their marriage in 1910. He even helped Itala while she was studying to take her midwifery exams in 1906, and she acknowledged Balzan's "great thoughtfulness" in this endeavour.

More financial and family woes came from his nephew Luigi Balzan, his brother Paolo's son, who had come to Milan hoping for a career as an opera singer. He began by asking for a loan in 1913. Balzan paid for his singing lessons and accommodations, on the agreement that Luigi go by a stage name, which the youth did. As Leone Leoni, he even got the bass part in *Aida* at the Teatro Dal Verme, another prestigious theatre in Milan. He went on a tournée in Japan and the company fell apart, so he had to ask his uncle to send him money so he could come home. That was not the last time. Once back to his hard life in Milan, Luigi continued to ask for help – "which I deserve for the name I bear" – almost blackmailing his uncle who was always ready to help him with generous 'perks' even when in exile in Switzerland.

Balzan was a generous man, especially with his daughter, although at a distance. Lina spent many years in a boarding school in Turin, where she got her diploma in 1909 and her teaching certification for elementary instruction at the Scuola Normale Femminile. In 1914 she got her university degree in French language teaching. In 1920, she took special courses for foreigners at the Gymnase in Lausanne. Balzan provided for her education with largesse, and kept her far away in boarding school, perhaps to protect her from the unexpected in life.

In 1927 Lina married Aldo Danieli, a career officer from Trento, hence always on the move. A sensitive, educated, genteel, refined woman, she had a stormy relationship with her husband, until he went to Africa as a volunteer. Then they separated, and Lina went back to Verona, in Balzan's native Veneto. During the war, she taught in a girls' school, the Collegio delle Fanciulle, in Milan.

Balzan's strong ties with the Veneto went deeper than his family and birthplace. This land, with its strong Catholic roots, instilled in him a profound respect for religious feast days – Christmas, Easter, the Assumption on 15 August – all marked by his sending gifts of traditional cakes and sweets – *panettoni*, *colombe* and *marrons glacés* – with the firm command that he should receive nothing in return. He was also very appreciative when his many friends remembered his saint's day, 30 December, a tradition in Italy that rivals birthday remembrances.

Another sign of his attachment to his native Veneto region were the friends of his youth, whom he kept all of his life. In Udine, Giuseppe Ridòmi and his wife and four children (including Cristano, who wrote a touching testimonial when Balzan died), were almost his second family, and he followed the children through their schooling and careers: it seems that Balzan admired the famliy's "happiness and harmony", and kept up a correspondence with them that is often full of humorous insights.

Balzan's goddaughter, Maria Bruna Lizza, married to Rosalindo Bassi, landowner from Cremona, was also from the Veneto. Balzan was very fond of their children, Francesco, Carla, Eugenia and especially Valentina, who strengthened these bonds by marrying Pio Ridòmi, from the abovementioned family that Balzan was so close to. There were also professional links, as with Vincenzo Fagiuoli, industrialist and paper-mill owner, who guided him and gave him advice on many occasions.

When he joined the staff of *Corriere*, a milieu of friendships with a strong 'regional' character let Balzan retain something of his Veneto roots throughout his Milanese period. At the beginning of the twentieth century, Milan was a bustling city in a phase of expansion, where social prestige and personal relationships were an indispensable point of departure.

CHAPTER THREE

# Life in Milan

In his more than thirty years at *Corriere della Sera*, Balzan spent his days tirelessly working in the historical centre of Milan, between Piazza Castello and the Galleria Vittorio Emanuele, and between the paper's headquarters in Via Solferino and La Scala. Immersed in an atmosphere of progress that had made Milan the most modern city in Italy, he immediately began to take part in the intense life of a centre that could boast of avant-garde art galleries, publishing houses and the most coveted opera house in the world. The social milieu in Milan was one of industry, business and finance, but there was also a lively intellectual climate.

The generation of Giuseppe Verdi was on its last legs. The composer had died in January 1901, and the new era of Arrigo Boito, Giacomo Puccini, Arturo Toscanini and Pietro Mascagni was about to begin. It was a time when the great publishing houses were thriving: Sonzogno, Ricordi, Treves, Vallardi and Hoepli. Milan was the city of the Futurists – Filippo Tommaso Marinetti, Giacomo Balla, Fortunato Depero and Umberto Boccioni – and their manifestos. Capital of the region of Lombardy, the city was also called the "moral capital" of Italy, and the pervading atmosphere of optimism at the beginning of the century attracted politicians, intellectuals, and industrialists, and made Milan a centre for the diffusion of the innovative ideas of a wealthy, dynamic urban upper class. As a result of his sense of commitment and tenacity, Balzan soon found a place in this city and became the right-hand man of the owners of *Corriere della Sera*.

Thanks to his hard work, he was on familiar terms with all of the big names in Via Solferino, the newspaper's headquarters: "My children and I would really enjoy having you over sometime for lunch", wrote Giulia Morbio, the widow of Benigno Crespi, one of the founders. The Albertinis also had words of esteem for him, and he was invited to their country house in the Piedmont region and to fashionable Milanese haunts with the elite of the world of journalism and culture. Once in high society, he attended events in the presence of the royal family.

Although Balzan had left his native Veneto region having very little experience in journalism, he was quick to carve out a respectable place for himself in society in just a few years. In rapid succession, he was decorated with the highest civic honours, which meant moving up in the ranks of society. Documents show how in all three cases, bureaucratic procedures were speeded up and everything resolved in his favour.

In 1910 he was granted the title of knight, receiving the parchment by decree of Vittorio Emanuele III in February. A year later, when he was already President of the Union of Newspaper Editors, a pronouncement on a promotion to Officer was applied for, and the nomination arrived on 13 March 1911. Another step up was the title of *commendatore*, with a decree of 4 April 1912. Three promotions in two years without having to wait for terms to expire was truly a record.

These honours are significant. In those years, they would have strengthened the ties between the Milanese daily paper and the conservative government of the centre right: the Prime Minister Antonio Salandra appointed *Corriere* owner Luigi Albertini senator in 1915, thus creating an even stronger tie between the State and the newspaper. In that period of *Corriere*'s history, when it was mouthpiece for the government line, Balzan was a mainstay; he got the 'battleship' running in tune with the instructions of the owners, and hence the ruling government. The decorations, of course, officially attest to his role in the management.

At home on the Milanese scene, Balzan reached his goals by other means, some of which also involved his passion for the performing arts, especially opera. In 1921, the corporation of La Scala was created, with Arturo Toscanini as music director. Balzan was nominated representative of the 'donors', as sponsors of the organization were called at the time.

This may have been the job Balzan enjoyed most, because it gave him an opportunity to bring musicians and artists together as his ancestors had, and cultivate the inborn Balzan love for the performing arts. These were the rare leisure time pursuits of a man for whom only a thin line divided work and life. The musicians Arrigo Boito and Umberto Giordano, and above all the orchestra conductor Arturo Toscanini were the personalities with whom he became acquainted.

There was also a coterie of friends who met in a private room of the posh Savini Restaurant in the Galleria Vittorio Emanuele downtown: the composer Giacomo Puccini, the writer Marco Praga, the theatre critic Renato Simoni and the playwrights Sabatino Lopez and Dario Niccodemi. Although these were fast friendships, the newspaper came between Balzan and his friends at times. There is a famous episode from the period when *Corriere* was sold out to less anti-Fascist owners, the Crespi family, in 1926. Since Toscanini already considered the paper philo-Fascist at that point, and was noted for his aversion to the regime, he cut off his subscription. Balzan was not a strong sympathizer of Fascism, but took his role at the paper so seriously that, although he was a close friend of Toscanini, he stopped speaking to him and referred to him as "that swine" like he usually did when angry with someone. Although they were both against the Fascists, Balzan took Toscanini's accusation against the newspaper as a personal offence.

For that matter, Balzan as manager was too entrenched in the paper to be able to separate it from his private life. In general he did not allow personal attacks, prejudices or interests to seep through what was published, but at times, his sympathies – guided by his passing mood – found an echo in the section with music and theatre reviews. People came to him seeking space in *Corriere*, powerful means to notoriety that the paper was.

Another clamorous instance of friction came about with the composer Giacomo Puccini, who felt he had been ignored or mistreated by the paper despite his acquired kinship with the owners of *Corriere*, through his marriage to one of their family members. Misunderstandings began in 1911, when the nationalist publication *Action Française* blocked the performance of Puccini's *La rondine*, which had been bought by the Italian publisher Sonzogno but ordered by 'enemy' Austrian publishers. Although commissioned before the war from 'authentic Italian' authors, the French newspaper threatened to cause a scandal. The affair had repercussions in Italian nationalist circles, and Puccini ended up on *Corriere*'s 'list'. Balzan may have been involved because he was supervisor of *Corriere*'s monthly supplement *La Lettura*, which continued to approve of the composer. "I think I deserve a little satisfaction," the irritated Puccini wrote to Balzan, "I've read that Sunday my *Trittico* will be performed at La Scala again. Good! I beg you to give a little consideration to the matter in your newspaper because I have not forgotten your critics' bilious comments on my works." Balzan had another opportunity to hear from Puccini in 1923, for another opera, *Gianni Schicchi*:

> My dear Balzan, please allow me to ask one question: why is everything that concerns me thrown away at

*Life in Milan*

*Corriere*? When *Schicchi* was performed in Paris in the autumn, Croci told me that he would send a story that was completely dedicated to me – it didn't come out in the paper – and now, a few days ago, the same thing happened in Vienna – it ended up in the waste basket... could you please inform me as to why this has happened? Surely you can understand how important *Corriere* is to me and how old my friendship with the family of our great paper is.

In this Balzan clearly let his personal life influence him in deciding what to print, and this only cooled off relations between the composer and the newspaper even more. "I am very sorry, but I cannot publish the note on Puccini," confided Balzan to *Corriere*'s music critic, "if you only knew how he behaved in Milan when *Nerone* was on, maligning it in every part, you would understand why we behave as we do." This work by the recently deceased Boito, Balzan's friend and another Veneto native from Padua, had been directed by Toscanini, but had not been well-received.

Balzan had not forgiven Puccini, and was waiting for a chance to make him pay. He managed to do so shortly thereafter, when involved in the negotiations for the billboard of the Scala in 1925. He put in an opera by Riccardo Zandonai rather than Puccini's *Turandot*. A musical critic of *Corriere*, who knew about the bad feelings between Balzan and Puccini, tried to mediate so as not to make the situation worse.

And in fact, Toscanini took it upon himself to direct the first world performance of Zandonai's *Cavalieri*. Only later would he direct *Turandot*. In any event, the change in programme was the last act in the old feud between Balzan and Puccini, who died in the meantime in Brussels on 29 November 1924, without ever seeing his new work performed at the Scala.

Despite these tenacious yet nonetheless rare grudges, Balzan's Achilles' heel was actually his reverence for his friendships. Balzan did not have many hard and fast friendships, and those he did have were for the most part from the *Corriere* family of journalists: Sabatino Lopez, Filippo Sacchi, Renato Simoni and Luigi Barbini. He remained loyal to them for his entire life, and even acted as executor of the writer Marco Praga's will. Yet however firm and fast his friendships might have been, he had a number of immediate enemies, and, since he was of a certain social standing in the management of a major Italian newspaper, he found that he had to be ready to resolve disputes through duels on various occasions, as was the custom at the time.

A journalist, especially if of a certain rank, had to be ready to answer personally for his writings, comments and attitudes. Despite the various challenges that he had to face, it must be said that Balzan nonetheless always managed to resolve problems without having to defend himself with weapons.

Several instances should nevertheless be noted. In the middle of the 1920s, Fascism was in power, with Mussolini set up as dictator. Fascist party officials wanted to get rid of Balzan, and so they accused him of plotting to sabotage *Corriere* together with the Albertinis. The *vice-podestà* of Milan, who wanted him out of the way, spread rumours that Balzan had used 'injurious language' against the Duce. Balzan himself unmasked the journalists who had tried to defame him. At this point, as was the custom, a challenge to a duel inevitably occurred. Balzan accepted the seconds of his adversaries and named his, while informing Arnaldo Mussolini so that he would in turn inform the Duce. It was through Mussolini's brother that the case was closed, but only for the moment, as it was to come up again several years later.

In another controversy, this time with a colleague, Balzan could not avoid seconds and courts of honour when it came to defending 'his' paper. The case was opened in the spring of 1930, when *La Stampa*, Turin's leading paper, was about to take the lead on *Corriere* because it started a literary prize, the Premio Letterario La Stampa. A journalist did waste time in attacking the Milanese paper with allusions to the local boys from the Veneto who worked there as reporters, and to the industrial interests of the Crespi brothers, the owners. Balzan was offended, and when he met the journalist in question, he challenged him with the classical slap in the face. The duel again was avoided only through the mediation of Arnaldo Mussolini.

Thus Balzan had few friends, but was pestered by many. A man who held such a position was besieged by dozens of troublemakers and insistent demands, and they would pursue him for years, becoming irritating and even dangerous. If not pandered to, they could really mean trouble! Not only journalists, but all sorts of petitioners as well – more or less well-known people who wanted a job. Hundreds of 'excellent men' asked for favours - officials, managers and politicians – and anonymous parties who would use the name Balzan because *Corriere* "united the authority of all of the Italian newspapers combined". Arnaldo Mussolini, director of *Il Popolo d'Italia*, often made his wishes clear and Balzan thus had the occasion to lend the Duce's brother a large sum of money so that he could improve the equipment of the 'president's' newspaper.

All sorts of people - writers and playwrights were no less diligent - approached him with the most varied requests, which was an unending source of vexation for this reserved man who had so many responsibilities. Never indulgent with indiscreet individuals, Balzan was generous instead with modest people, especially if they were or ill or afflicted. He always made constant, considerable gifts to the most varied charitable institutions, agencies and associations. The list of recipients goes from the national organization to help veterans, to charitable institutions, to the opera season at the Arena in Verona and the symphonic orchestra in Milan.

Thus he became a capable businessman who had relations with dozens of institutions and organizations, and in his name registered shares were designated to go towards the increasingly high salaries that would place him in a privileged category of the work force. He also made his mark in speculating on foreign currencies. Over the years, Balzan's profit-sharing in industry was developed by his great ability to manage money and handle relations with bankers and business leaders. His economic and social position made things easy. His lifestyle, however, gave birth to the legend of "extreme thriftiness and moderation." This was also true as far as his workplace was concerned: an "unpretentious, sparsely furnished office", next to the cashier's window. And the same was true of his private quarters: he lived in public housing, but he had everything he needed or wanted. He was an elegant, refined man. His suits were from Prandoni, the renowned tailor downtown in Piazza San Fedele. He smoked original *toscano* cigars, and went to the best restaurants, despite a special diet for stomach problems. He had a box for the opera and concert season at the Scala, and lavished his friends with expensive gifts. Luigi Barzini, Jr. remembers one of his expensive habits:

> My grandmother was from Venice – a small, very lively woman, capricious and very friendly. They only talked in dialect – the dialect of Goldoni that may have reminded her of her youth. He often went by taxi to visit her on Sunday afternoons. (Balzan never had, as I remember, his own car). He let the taxi wait for him for hours, while the metre ticked off exorbitant amounts. This habit, in frugal times, seemed to all of us a maharajah's extravagance, and filled us with respect. It was, after all, the only way he let himself enjoy his riches.

Every now and then, Balzan needed a break from his work and responsibilities, and so took short vacations or breaks to

*Life in Milan*

take care of his health. He usually went to Sanremo on the Italian Riviera, or to spas like Montecatini, Brennerbad or other places in the Swiss Alps. In short, Balzan led a typical upper class life, according to the social canons in force since the beginning of the twentieth century, with its myth of progress and the conviction that these objectives would be met and its balance never be thrown off. Milan offered its bourgeois elite class all of the fashionable cultural pleasures that any European city could – like Berlin, London, Paris or Moscow. Moreover, there was a sense of optimism that a long period of at least fifty years of peace on the continent was about to begin. But those social canons were soon to be overthrown by political events and their dramatic consequences.

CHAPTER FOUR
# Mussolini Arrives on the Scene

The First World War, in which Italy was involved from 1915-18, marked a clean break with the liberal era. Involvement in the conflict had tremendous consequences: loss of human lives, social and political demands on the part of the masses and veterans from the front, and the clash between Socialist and Catholic groups and between conservatives and combatants. After 1919, all of these factions ended up under the aegis of nationalism and Fascism with their leading exponents: the poet and writer Gabriele D'Annunzio and the journalist and rabble-rouser Benito Mussolini, in competition to bring down the old bourgeois-liberal order and set up a new regime. After three years of disorder and violence, the Fascists were in power.

On 27 October 1922, the night before the March on Rome, Benito Mussolini was still in Milan, where he lived and where the headquarters of his newspaper, *Il Popolo d'Italia*, was located. He was about to publish the plan for the Fascist Insurrection, and his thugs were making the rounds of the major daily newspapers in Milan to make sure they did not get in their way. At *Corriere* they found Balzan, who was not considered hostile to the regime, but who stated that he would pass the message on. While Italy was waiting for the news with bated breath, Mussolini met Balzan in one of Milan's major theatres, the Dal Verme, for a confidential exchange of points of view on the political crisis. In short, he wanted to know how *Corriere* was going to act.

On the 28th, the day of the insurrection, *Corriere* director Luigi Albertini, who was against Mussolini as head of this "not yet triumphal uprising", published a negative article on the risk of a coup, and it was seen as an attack on Mussolini's rough necks. The Milan commando of the Fascist forces decreed "suppression" of the newspaper. Since Albertini saw this act as an affront to guaranteed "freedom of speech and opinion," he decided simply not to print the newspaper on the 29th. This was an outright act of dissent, and so Mussolini, once in power, began to attack the owners of *Corriere*, trying to get rid of the Albertini brothers and replace them with more politically aligned owners, the Crespi family.

It took the Fascists three years to oust the Albertini family, and during these three years, both the owners and the management were under continuous pressure. Balzan, as the one who "passed on" orders, unwillingly became a leading figure in the battle for *Corriere* in a period of siege that coincided with the clash between liberal-democrats, socialists and those who were against the Fascists and their allies.

After an almost peaceful interval, hostility towards the Albertini-owned *Corriere* began again with a vengeance in 1924-25, at first in the province and then in Milan during the crisis that followed the murder of the socialist member of Parliament Giacomo Matteotti by the Fascists in Rome (10 June 1924), and then after the "liberticidal" laws that no longer guaranteed basic civil liberties like freedom of speech, of the press and of association. Balzan spoke out in defence of the paper, and we have already seen the consequences this had for *Corriere*, with the sell-out to the Crespi family and Balzan's personal

## Mussolini Arrives on the Scene

involvement in the transaction. All of this happened at a time of extreme tension: Fascism had not yet secured a firm hold, the relations between Mussolini and the *ras*, the fascist political bosses in the provinces, were still under discussion and the opposition had not yet been annihilated by any means.

On 25 January 1924, the king signed a decree that dissolved Parliament and called for elections on 6 April. The Fascist squads took advantage of these months to intimidate or strike adversaries so as to obtain the majority at the polls and two thirds of Parliament according to the Acerbo Law, which was forced through Parliament expressly for the purpose. Among opposition newspapers, *Corriere* was the first to pay the price, since all copies of the paper were seized in centres in Lombardy and in the Veneto where the Fascists proved to be more hotheaded. With "blunt objectivity", Balzan explained the facts to Mussolini, certain that he would be the first to "condemn them" and "give severe orders".

The Fascists in Udine began to destroy copies of *Corriere*, so Balzan sent Mussolini another petition in which he condemned not so much the momentary damage to the newspaper as the effects that it would have on the public. Thus, on the eve of the elections, Mussolini ordered the head of the Police to "stop acts of vandalism", perhaps to avoid contestation. The truce did not last long: the Milanese Fascists, unhappy about election results, attacked *Corriere* for its lack of participation in the electoral campaign, blaming the paper for its enormous responsibility for the fall in votes with respect to 1922. A Fascist faction pressed charges against Balzan, and in May he resigned as head of the editors' union, but at least on the surface tried to stay in Mussolini's good graces because at that time in Italy, everything depended on the Duce's will.

The newspaper, like other mouthpieces of the opposition, regained power in the summer of 1924, while the murder of Matteotti, attributed to Mussolini's hit men, weakened the government and even the squads themselves. At the end of June, with Balzan's resignation, *Corriere* left the editors' union. In the meantime, the economist Luigi Einaudi wrote from the pages of the paper, sternly reprimanding the "captains of the Italian economy" for not speaking out. Giovanni Amendola, head of *Corriere*'s Roman office, was also struck by the squads.

This sudden move by the opposition was not forgotten by the extremist Fascist fringes, which shortly thereafter got the upper hand in the provinces and imposed their systems on Mussolini. On 4 November 1924, the anniversary of the WWI victory of 1918, incidents broke out all over Italy between Fascists and liberal democrat veterans of the First World War. In Milan, the riots resulted in new episodes of violence. Balzan was among the victims, taking a beating by a group of thugs from the Fascist squads in the Galleria Vittorio Emanuele in the centre of Milan.

But he considered it an isolated case that was connected more with the newspaper than with him as an individual, and did not come out with a public statement against Fascism or the head of the government. On the contrary, during the transactions to oust the Albertini family, he consolidated his relations with moderate Fascist circles, where he had influential friends who counted, like Augusto Turati, member of a Fascist squad and future secretary of the party. When the transfer of property from the Albertini to the Crespi family imposed by the Duce was concluded in 1925, Balzan continued to hold his position as managing director of the publishing firm of *Corriere della Sera*. Why? It may have been his ambition. As noted by Albertini, Balzan "in his heart of hearts longed to extend his authority to policy-making and the editorial office." In any event, the company breathed a sigh of relief at his decision to stay, and this is also because a wing of the National Fascist Party did not approve of the paper's non-committal nature and the lack of "immediate Fascistization".

Another step in the direction of suppressing freedom of the press came in 1926. The world of journalism was topsy-turvy,

## Mussolini Arrives on the Scene

especially in management at *Il Secolo*, *Corriere*'s main competitor. At *Corriere*, the intellectual and art critic Ugo Ojetti became director. Balzan once again was under fire: "It happened," he wrote, "that when the Albertini brothers left the scene, while I endeavoured in every way to make sure there would not be a shake-up at the paper, working more and more intensely to all possible limits – day and night, even Christmas Day, trying to make the tasks of the Director easier in every way, without ever invading his territory – while I did all of this, I heard people accusing me of trying to take the director's place". Years later, Alberto Albertini wrote:

> There was indeed a man inside there who was driven by an iron will to rule; but he had no official power over the editorial staff, and he was the very one that the editorial staff opposed. I'm talking about the manager Balzan. The strife between this man and the disrupted, recalcitrant editorial staff was over the Crespi family and Croci, and characterised the first period of *Corriere* without the Albertini brothers. Here I confess, and not without true regret, that I refused to report stories from this time. There was plenty of material; the characters were all there: the Crespi family, Croci, Balzan, Ojetti, all the others. I can see them, I know them by heart, I could portray them in their psychologies, in their actions, in their voices and gestures – against the background of ambitions, hesitations and fears, accusations and counter-accusations, ingenuousness and dirty tricks, of Mussolini judging from Rome and sending out mandates – of Farinacci ranting and raving from Cremona because *Corriere* had not instantaneously become Fascist.

The atmosphere at the newspaper did not improve, and Ojetti wrote: "The truth is that here at *Corriere*, there are only a few cordial Fascistophiles among us" – editors and reporters could have cared less. Balzan had to maintain the standards of the paper high. His strategy: hire the most famous reporters from his competitors, save journalists with liberal standpoints and start up attractive columns. There are numerous documented cases: when the journalist Paolo Monelli resigned from Mondadori's *Il Secolo,* Balzan was the one to make the acquisition easier, saying "glad you're part of the *Corriere* family." When another journalist, Filippo Sacchi, who had been sent to various countries in Europe after 1914, was ousted from *Corriere* in 1926, sent to Australia as a correspondent and then eventually fired because he was a true antifascist, Balzan found a way to give him work by inventing a column. Created especially for this friend, the *Rassegna cinematografica* film review turned out to be one of the paper's most successful columns.

Thus, out on a ledge in the battle to defend *Corriere*'s leadership, Balzan found that he was denounced in rival papers as anti-Fascist, on the pretext of the newspaper's lukewarm, noncommittal stance towards Fascism. The attack coincided with Fascist measures to 'normalise' the press – reduce the number of pages and standardise the price – as decreed by Mussolini's government. This was apparently a technical move aimed at striking *Corriere* politically. Balzan left for Rome, and the Crespi family went with him to negotiate with the Duce. And so amidst difficulties and complications, Balzan stayed on as *ad interim* director and found he had to deal with public relations, while work built up after Ojetti was fired and his substitute arrived.

In December 1927, "year VI of the Fascist era", a new director was sent to Milan: Maffio Maffii, a 'blackshirt', and former head of Mussolini's press office. He stayed two years. Balzan got on well with him. Correspondence in the *Corriere* archives shows that Maffii did not make any decisions without consulting Balzan first. It even turned out that Maffii did not have the power to hire Fascist reporters because Balzan was always against him "for some reason or another". One source writes:

1. Eugenio Balzan at *Corriere della Sera*, 1926 (International Balzan Foundation Archives, Milan).

**2**. Eugenio Balzan's father, Lorenzo (International Balzan Foundation Archives, Milan).
**3**. Eugenio Balzan's mother, Angelina (International Balzan Foundation Archives, Milan).

**4**. Eugenio Balzan's nurse Ermenegilda Previera in Masi, Rovigo (International Balzan Foundation Archives, Milan).
**5**. Eugenio Balzan with friends (International Balzan Foundation Archives, Milan).

**6**. Eugenio Balzan as a young man (Private Archive Riccardo Luzzatto, Milan).
**7**. Eugenio Balzan's brother Luigi, geologist and explorer, 1888 (Museo Civico Baruffaldi, Badia Polesine).

8. Eugenio Balzan as a soldier in the Savoia Cavalleria, 1893 (Centro Documentazione *Corriere della Sera*, Milan).

**9**. On the Way to Canada, 1901 (Centro Documentazione *Corriere della Sera*, Milan).

**10**. Eugenio Balzan's daughter Lina with her mother, 1900 (International Balzan Foundation Archives, Milan).

**11**. Eugenio Balzan's daughter Lina with her mother, 1910 (International Balzan Foundation Archives, Milan).

12. Eugenio Balzan at *Corriere della Sera* (International Balzan Foundation Archives, Milan).

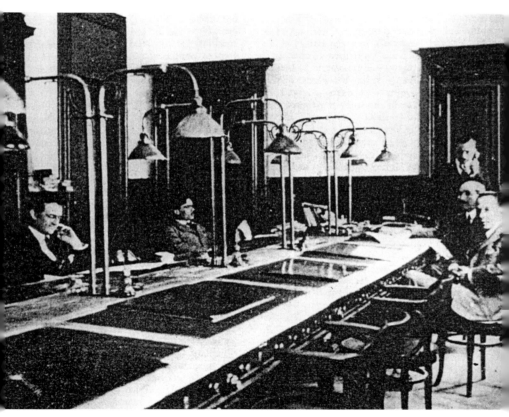

13. The conference room (now Sala Albertini) at *Corriere della Sera* in the 1920s (Centro Documentazione *Corriere della Sera*, Milan).

14. Giacomo Puccini in the 1920s (Centro Documentazione *Corriere della Sera*, Milan).

15. Eugenio Balzan on a walk in the mountains near St. Moritz (Switzerland) in the 1940s (Private Archive Zighetti Bassi, Varese).

16. Applause for Arturo Toscanini and the La Scala Orchestra after the inaugural concert at the renovated La Scala theatre in Milan on 11 May, 1946 (Centro Documentazione *Corriere della Sera*, Milan).

**17.** Eugenio Balzan in Venice after WWII, 1948 (Private Archive Marco Fisch, Lugano).

18. Eugenio Balzan in Lugano in the 1950s (Private Archive Gina Alani, Zurich).

**19.** Eugenio Balzan's niece Paola Pilogallo, who first had the idea of creating the Balzan Foundation (Private Archive Riccardo Luzzatto, Milan).

**20.** Lina Balzan in Gardone with her friends, March 1955 (Private Archive Laura Racca Sartori, Milan).

**21.** Eugenio Balzan's daughter Lina Balzan, 1956, the person who created the Balzan Foundation (International Balzan Foundation Archives, Milan).

"In order to have an idea of what Eugenio meant to *Corriere*, it is enough to say that when the Crespi brothers went to see him, they stood while he talked to them and explained things from his comfortable rocking chair." And another: "Balzan was the one who had the muscle power [...] rumour had it that there were serious differences of opinion with the Crespi family, and that Balzan managed *Corriere* as he saw fit [...]for them he was indispensable [...] they were such milktoasts [...] at the end of the year all they wanted was their money."

By that time, Balzan was the head of *Corriere* – virtually the director. He had just turned fifty, had influential friends, and was at the height of his career. He seemed irremovable. "Newspaper editors," it was noted, "with their boorish sense of humour, said that after the Albertini brothers had left nothing changed at all, except that while they were there, the manager went upstairs to talk to the director, while now it was the director who had to go downstairs to talk to the manager." Balzan's 'veto' as managing director, and indirectly the veto of the owners, the Crespi family, acted as a sort of barrier against outsiders' meddling with the paper's independence.

True to his nature, Balzan was careful with touchy cases, especially if respectable people were involved. If tensions arose, it was because of reporters who were 'too' Fascist, or who were hard to control because they were protected. Trouble came from a few 'difficult' correspondents. This was the case with Luigi Barzini, Sr., *Corriere*'s star reporter, famous for covering the Paris-Beijing motor rally and for the *Corriere d'America* project in Dallas in 1923. He had pulled strings from the United States to go in place of the director Croci, and subsequently of the director Ojetti, which was not well received at *Corriere* headquarters in Milan. Despite all this, there was a certain willingness to give Barzini a position in management. Months later, at a difficult time for the firm, Balzan made him an offer once again, but in the end, nothing came of it.

With the progressive "Fascistization" of the press, Balzan also took it upon himself to defend reporters who had fallen into disfavour. Contacts, compromises and friendships were used in the attempt to save the most precarious: if there were purges of editors suspected of being "lukewarm" towards the regime, Balzan – and thus indirectly the Crespi family – stepped in for some of them with the power of "veto". The situation became more complicated when it came to covering General Umberto Nobile's expedition to the North Pole.

Here it is worth mentioning that dirigibles were the only means of transatlantic air transport at the time – the first transatlantic flight was Lindbergh's in 1927, and there was great competition to show that Italy's aeronautic industry had what it took. Relying on the success of the Norge, which Nobile had designed and piloted to the North Pole with an international crew in 1926, he proposed a new, solely Italian expedition in 1927. In these years of great progress in transatlantic air transport, this was a great opportunity for propaganda for Mussolini. As noted by one of *Corriere*'s antagonists, *L'Impero*, the Duce was "always ready to claim and defend Italy's valour." The undertaking, in which various clans of Fascist party officials wanted to have their part, brought about string-pulling and schemes for financing, and started controversies among newspapers in order to have exclusive press coverage, which *Corriere* thought it had secured with the embarkation on the flight of the reporter Cesco Tomaselli.

"Under Balzan and Maffii, *Corriere* thought the paper had exclusive coverage in the bag after having invested millions in the undertaking," recalls Glauco Licata in his history of *Corriere della Sera*. However, *Il Popolo d'Italia* had also managed to put one of its reporters, Ugo Lago, on board, and obtain exclusive rights from Stefani, the official press agency, to sell stories abroad. Thus for *Corriere*, the operation turned out to be more difficult than planned. The *podestà* of Milan, Ernesto

## Mussolini Arrives on the Scene

Belloni; the vice, Morgagni; Arnoldo Mondadori; the director of *Il Popolo d'Italia*, Arnaldo Mussolini; the administrator, Giulio Barella – all took part in the new *querelle*.

Once the sum to be raised had been decided upon, the committee financing the operation asked Mondadori about books and film, and Balzan about the press. Negotiations took months, and an agreement was reached in 1928. The expedition ended catastrophically, with the death of various members of the expedition, including the reporter from *Il Popolo d'Italia*. After the disaster, the association of newspaper editors suggested that the news service of *Corriere* be considered "a national news service". Balzan seized the opportunity and fronted the expenses to his envoy , but without detracting the sum from what *Corriere* owed to the committee: complications arose with Rome, so that the affair which already led to the director Ojetti's getting the sack, under the pretext that he had neglected the expedition, caused Balzan to be blamed.

The case against Ojetti was launched in 1927 by *L'Impero*, which had criticized *Corriere* for not acknowledging their reporter's coverage - the only one to credit Italy with the exploit - of the Norge expedition of the previous year. And so Ojetti was off-handedly replaced by Maffii. Then it was Balzan's turn. While he went back and forth between Milan and the capital in order to try and save journalists excluded from the professional registers, *L'Impero* attacked him directly. Why?

*L'Impero* was aware that abovementioned "injurious language" that had got Balzan into trouble with Mussolini and nearly led to a duel in the mid-20s was back in circulation again. His precise words were supposedly, "They should build a monument to the strumpet who gave Mussolini syphilis." With the reappearance of the old accusation, there was clearly a 'campaign' against him, but this time his reputation was being dragged before the entire country. His honesty was at stake. He had to fight to make the truth known in public, and at the very time when the crisis of the Nobile expedition was taking place. In an interview with "an eminent colleague in Rome", Balzan had discovered that the *vicepodestà* of Milan had repeated the old slur on the Duce two years after the "ugly incident". When he connected the short article that had appeared in *L'Impero* with what he knew, he appealed to the secretary of the *fascio* in Milan to open a new investigation.

The dispute, which he thought had been closed by a court of honour in 1926, was opened again in 1928, with renewed interest in 'setting things straight'. Arnaldo Mussolini supported Balzan again. The case seemed to be closed, but then after a few months, it started up again. An almost obsessive interest in clearing up details, which would seem more like a personal grievance, were actually part of the usual hostility of extremist Fascist circles towards *Corriere*. In fact, months before, Arnaldo had suggested that the Duce receive the Crespi family, *Corriere*'s new owners, along with Balzan, because they were being attacked for administrative matters. Thus, creating a scandal around Balzan was the way to destroy the paper. And every opportunity – including the 'injurious language' – was taken to achieve this goal.

How did the owners of *Corriere* react to the ordeals that the firm was going through? In order to ease pressure, the Crespi family made 'donations' of "gifts of inland revenue and for large families" with the considerable sum of one million Lire in 1928. Balzan was the intermediary for the new owners, and his colleague Arnaldo Mussolini, for the Duce. The opportunity was immediately seized upon, as is shown by a feverish exchange of telegrams between Rome and Milan. The Duce thanked the Crespi family, and after this first enormous payoff, Arnaldo would have other occasions to make sure such "spontaneous gifts" reached Rome from *Corriere* headquarters in Via Solferino 28.

## Mussolini Arrives on the Scene

Thus the Crespi family had paid the toll, and could at least insist on their good faith with Arnaldo Mussolini. According to them, it was not the task of the deputy secretary of the Corporations, Giuseppe Bottai, to censor journalists, but rather, of the Prime Minister, the Minister of the Interior or of the Press Office of the head of the government. "A Triumph of Compromise" – this is how that particular moment in the middle of 1928 was defined by the Fascist party official Roberto Farinacci, director of rival Cremona newspaper *Regime fascista*, and one of the ring-leaders in ousting the Albertini brothers from *Corriere della Sera*.

Of course, the combined gift of one million Lire from the Crespi family and Balzan guaranteed *Corriere* almost one year of respite, but then a changing of the guard was imposed on the director's office. In 1929, Balzan came to know that there was "something going on in high places" at high levels in the main newspapers. At *Corriere*, in fact, Maffii was replaced by Aldo Borelli. But Balzan remained at the helm as managing director. Former director of Florence's *La Nazione*, Borelli was one who would compromise between the old liberal style and what Mussolini called the 'Fascist style'. But Balzan remained at the helm of Corriere, and the atmosphere was still 'Albertinian', with the paper's traditional expectations for keeping strictly to work hours, diligence and an almost maniacal drive for precision. For that matter, this tradition was not very permeable to Fascism, and so continued to irritate the Duce. Despite the fact that he was not at all passionate about Fascism, Borelli remained at *Corriere* headquarters in Via Solferino until Mussolini's fall on 25 July 1943.

And Balzan? His power began to decline. He had had many responsibilities. Ojetti, who was often absent, had left him to deal with Fascist aggression alone. Maffii, after "two or three gorgeous *gaffes* that earned him the nickname Gaffio Gaffii, [a pun on his name Maffio Maffii]", depended on him for everything. As for the Crespi family, who stayed outside the milieu of the newspaper, they had appointed Balzan as administrator of their affairs. In Borelli, instead, Balzan found an ally and a friend, but the duties of the two men were separate. While *Corriere* was on the way towards 'normalization' – that is, towards complete subjugation to the regime – for some individuals, Balzan was the last obstacle to their plans, mainly because he did not give anti-fascist reporters the sack.

Borelli stood by Balzan. In one instance, in order to "appease the regime" after another "quarrel" that Balzan had had at the Scala over political matters with one of the Fascist party officials, Borelli presented the Duce with plans for instituting a Benito Mussolini Prize at the Accademia d'Italia – with aims of patching things up for the paper. *Corriere* would publish the rules and regulations for the ceremony at the Quirinale, in the presence of the king and queen, every 21 April, commemorating "the birth of Rome." Balzan himself would make sure that the 1931 prize was awarded to writer and colleague Ada Negri.

But there was no peace for him or for *Corriere*. *L'Impero* of Rome attacked Balzan once again when, since he was the most authoritative executive of the paper, he did not give adequate coverage to a violent episode in which a young Fascist had been wounded. Borelli covered him, writing that Balzan "had nothing to do with the production and political orientation" of the paper, because he, Borelli, was the director, and hence policy-maker.

Borelli's actions also emphasized his agreement with Balzan in terms of relations with the Duce, too. For Christmas of 1930, Balzan paid a considerable sum of money to the legions of the Militia, and the Crespi family made a generous donation "for various charitable purposes in the city of Milan". This in itself did not protect *Corriere* from the aggression of *L'Impero*, which continued to make ill-concealed accusations against the

## Mussolini Arrives on the Scene

Milan daily paper and, again, Balzan. Borelli stepped in, but had been informed that there were plans in certain circles to "get rid of Balzan" and fascisticize the administration of *Corriere*, possibly by inventing a scandal.

Balzan's position became even weaker after the sudden death of Arnaldo Mussolini (21 December 1931). Throughout their long friendship, Arnaldo had protected him in many difficult moments. Only a few months earlier had Balzan made the umpteenth donation, together with the Crespi family, in memory of Arnaldo's son, who had died very young. It was the end of an era. The Duce had lost his brother - the only person he could trust; others like Balzan lost a moderate individual who had often acted as intermediary between the dictator and the more factionist sectors of the regime.

Only a few months after Arnaldo's death, yet another "confidential" dossier arrived on Mussolini's desk. An informer of the regime's political Police had given the Duce the news that a journalist had sensitive information about Balzan. It was a plot to oust Balzan and his protégés at *Corriere*.

To ease the tension, the Crespi family 'donated' more money as 'charity' to the city in 1932, through *Il Popolo d'Italia*. The association of newspaper editors had in the meantime awarded Balzan a gold medal for merit. A brief ceasefire, then a more intense assault began on the newspaper and on the "liberaloid" political line that "had always characterised it", with the aim of first distancing Borelli in order to isolate and then eliminate Balzan. In 1933, as soon as Borelli was included in a list of nominations for senator, there was an attempt to discredit him for having married the Russian dancer-coreographer in exile, Jia Ruskaya (Evghenia Borisenko), about whom many unfounded rumours circulated.

In the meantime, news of shake-ups at the management level of the press, especially at *Corriere*, hit the newspapers in Paris. In fact at the end of the year, OVRA, the Fascist secret police, sent out warnings that it would be better to have an avowed Fascist in place of the director of *Corriere* in the nominations for senator. The substitution would be the opportunity the Fascists had been waiting for for so long. The report went straight to the Duce, but it got there too late, because – mysteriously – Balzan had already been missing from his office in via Solferino for months.

CHAPTER FIVE

# Life in Switzerland

" *Commendatore* Balzan left *Corriere* on 11 May 1933", as was noted on a sheet of stationery with the newspaper letterhead. The key post that he had occupied for over thirty years was vacant, this time for months, but the newspaper – as was insinuated in the highest levels of the government – continued to be guided by Balzan. No one knew where he was – only the director Aldo Borelli and very few others knew that the managing director was in a hotel in Switzerland, officially for "his health". He did not return to Italy until 1946, after the fall of Fascism and the end of the War. They were years of solitude, in self-imposed 'exile'.

At first it seemed as though his absence would only be temporary, like any of those periods when he had gone in for treatments for stomach problems in the past. At *Corriere,* however, more precise information was on hand, and Borelli, who knew he was at the Hotel Saratz in Pontresina, telephoned him often and went to visit him. Borelli was requested by the powers that be to "continue to compile our fine *Corriere* as usual," even if many collaborators were not at their posts. But those who sweated it out were the owners. And so when Aldo and Mario Crespi went to Pontresina, Balzan informed them of his decision to ask for a leave of absence.

One senses that it was not simply a matter of therapy, but that something else was really the problem. The political Police had collected rumours on his long stay in Switzerland, and it was evidently not for health reasons. The old 'defamation' against Mussolini – the nightmare that he was never able to rid himself of – was brought up again. It was time he be able to live in peace, but with the seasonal closing of the hotels, the convalescent Balzan had to move to Zurich, to a clinic specializing in stomach ailments.

His health seemed to improve, and when friends arrived from Italy they found him in quiet surroundings. In 1934, in fact, at headquarters in Via Solferino, his imminent return was discussed. The Crespi were sure of it. Instead, Balzan began to withdraw. He received severance pay and never set foot in Italy again. He had even made arrangements to start various rumours: "I don't feel like going on with a regime that does not allow freedom of the press and so I am retiring [...] nor can I say that I am pleased about how Italy is being run. I am old and alone, I will retire in Switzerland, but I am doing so decently, and without harming anyone. I have waited all these years to see if some way to live might not be found: there is none".

His leaving the country can be related to the fall of his political protector Augusto Turati, former secretary of the Fascist party who had fallen into disgrace because of the manoeuvring of rival provincial party officials. This is a conceivable motive. The managing director of *Corriere*, in "a very depressed physical condition", became ill because of "unjust treatment" by the Italian authorities – in short, "a case of nerves". How could he *not* be in such a state? For years he had been the target of intimidation, threats and provocation. It is no wonder that the consequences went along with him to peaceful Switzerland. Back and forth between clinics and hotels, it was the beginning of a secluded life, quite different from his years at *Corriere* headquarters in Via Solferino. He was sixty, and had received substantial severance pay. He had financial interests in Switzerland, and from that point on wanted only to take care of his estate.

Ever since Fascist power came onto the scene in 1922, he had asked that dividends and bonuses (commissions on increases in profit sharing) be paid in Swiss Francs in Switzerland, withdrawn from the proceeds from sales of *Corriere* in the Swiss Confederation, in particular, proceeds from the very popular Sunday paper, *Domenica del Corriere*. Administered with discernment, those considerable earnings constituted considerable assets, which then became a fortune since he had invested his severance pay in 1934 in shares with the Swiss firm Nestlé.

Another aspect to link to his not wanting to repatriate, and to this handling of millions, comes from this circumstance: the three Crespi brothers – owners of *Corriere*, of textile industries and electrical companies – also had enormous assets abroad. At a time when special laws regulated how capital abroad was to be declared, they had put all of their property in Balzan's name in Switzerland, charging him with the responsibility of administering it for them, but in his name.

But did he really carry on in this position as private administrator? It would be an original interpretation. It is certain that Balzan regularly and competently dealt with the fiscal aspects of the investments of various credit institutions, and he absolutely had no thought of returning to Italy. He moved to the Hotel Schweizerhof in Zurich. Then, because of the climate, went down to Lugano with the intention of stopping off at the Hotel Bristol. And it was there that the problems began. Balzan had entered Switzerland with a valid passport. Hence, he was neither a political exile nor an illegal immigrant. However, in order to set up residence in the country, he had to deal with the red tape that was compulsory at the time for foreigners who had intentions of staying on Swiss soil.

With the massive influx of refugees from Nazi Germany,

especially those who were subject to racial persecution, Switzerland had modified its legislation on foreigners, who were tolerated for an initial period of three months. After 1933 the federal law on residence and stay gave the Cantons the power to grant 'permits' of up to two years to those who were not engaged in "lucrative activities". In order to stay, Balzan availed himself of this 'permit to stay', which was granted by the Cantonal Police of Zurich and of Ticino. When his two-year permit had expired in 1935 in Zurich he went to Lugano, and in 1937 he did a stint in France and then returned again in 1938.

This moving around let him get around the heavy taxes of the city of Zurich, among other things. The Ticinese gendarmerie let him get his cantonal permit for Zurich each time he needed it. For the first years, he had to make do as best he could. He tried to solve his residence problems in 1939 by asking for citizenship, in order to live the autumn of his life as a Swiss citizen, but he ended up not making a final decision. He simply established permanent residence in Zurich, but without taking any further measures to "naturalize".

Trouble came from Italy. He led a reserved, almost mysterious life, always prudent and respectful of foreigners' consignments "not to engage in politics and not to damage Swiss neutrality". But in 1936, OVRA, the Fascist secret police, informed Rome of his habits and encounters with Italians, and this led the Swiss government to open an investigation. Their surveillance reports show us the daily life of a singular individual: well-off, discreet, a creature of habit, solitary but with important friends, indifferent to politics but watchful and informed. And always with a newspaper under his arm: *Corriere della Sera*.

In 1938 the legal authorities in Berne asked the Canton gendarmerie in Bellinzona for information on two of the Hotel Bristol's guests in Lugano, including Balzan, "this last individual highly suspected of espionage". The gendarmerie ruled out the charge of espionage: Balzan was in Switzerland "because of differences of opinion with the regime," and was not "an active anti-Fascist but simply one who, indifferent to such matters, wanted to live in peace [...] He was wise to move all of his assets to Switzerland and elsewhere, because they generate revenues that let him to live like a lord. He does not go to Italy, nor does he want to because he knows he will have problems with high level Fascists. And he does not appear to be a sympathizer. He is not afraid of ambushes and is ready to challenge any attempt to plot against his person."

*Diskrete Überwachung* in the Cantons of Lucerne and Zurich in the periods when he stayed in those cities followed him with Swiss precision. In any event, the Zurich police continued to watch him as a suspect, on an almost hourly basis. But the most precise notices were collected from the innkeeper from Verona of the "Accademia-Posthof" in Zurich, where Balzan usually had lunch. Loquacious and well-informed, the innkeeper said that he had known Balzan for five or six years; that he knew he resided at the Bristol in Lugano; that he was a millionaire; that he had a collection of paintings in Milan that was worth several million; that he had already been to Switzerland in the past for health reasons - "stomach problems". He also said that he knew that Balzan no longer went to Italy because of "something" against Fascism, and that he thought he was "an extremely polite individual" whom he would "swear by".

What then was the world of Balzan like at this time? While many were making a fuss about him for one reason or another, he kept up his habitual relationships, albeit with a certain degree of anxiety. In the summer he stayed in Engadina. When in the Canton Ticino, he surrounded himself with the few new friends he had made and contacted official representatives of Italy in Berne and Zurich.

The newly accredited Minister Plenipotentiary Attilio Tamaro paid his respects, "if I can be of help to you in Rome, I am without a doubt at your service." Balzan was also assured of a diplomatic channel between Berne and Milan, which at times he called into action in favour of Italians who had fallen upon hard times. He had a few, but enduring, female friendships, and saw his daughter several times, including 1939, when Lina was in Lausanne for medical treatments.

His circle in Lugano was homey, almost a clan of trustworthy individuals whom he could count on: authorities for paperwork; friends with Italian roots whom he could feel at ease with; executives to help with managing his estate – people who reassured him, like his colleague Luigi Caglio, the chemist Giovanni Bordoni, the lawyers Carlo Battaglini and Pier Carlo Nobile, the banking consultants Sergio Colombi, Arturo Lang and Carlo Pernsch, the police official Enrico Camponovo, Colonel Giuseppe Albisetti, the Italian diplomat and political exile Rino De Nobili, and his very dear friend, the dentist Federico Fisch with his sister Amarilli and her sons Marco and Ugo. For an embittered and very solitary Balzan, the Fisch home in Via Dufour 9 in Lugano would continue to be a touchstone until his death.

On 1 September 1939, the Second World War began, and on 10 June 1940, Italy entered the war. For neutral Switzerland, these were years of international and domestic tension, as well as a state of alert because of the threat of a German invasion in the border areas. Should such an invasion have happened, it would have meant dividing the country between the Reich and Italy. Foreigners were watched, the press was censored and intelligence services were activated to avoid unpleasant surprises. In a note on wiretapping between Switzerland and Italy in 1941 there was still talk of Balzan and his contacts. A year later, another report from well-informed sources stated that it was known that, in his comings and goings to and from Zurich, the "self-styled emigrant" Balzan supposedly exchanged "important information" with Tamaro, nominated by the Fascist regime. Thus doubts were raised because he supposedly had relations with the minister and with the consul of Italy, despite the fact that he had had 'problems' with Fascism.

Then nothing. The surveillance ceased, and Balzan went back to being another foreign *rentier* in Switzerland. He seemed to live the years that followed – which were among the most tragic for the entire world – peacefully, except for his health problems. And he defended this peace and quiet by using *Corriere* as a shield. He had his correspondence forwarded to Via Solferino in Milan, and from there, a representative saw to sending it to him in Switzerland. The trick worked, and his secrecy was guaranteed. His friend Arnaldo Sartori wrote to his daughter Lina Balzan:

> He telephoned me from wherever he was almost every day and even more than once a day – and always at least once a month, at times every week, I went to see him in Berne, Zurich, Lucerne and lately in Lugano. In short, I continued to be his secretary for the twenty years he was abroad.

Occasional encounters with Italians appeared to bring Balzan back to life again. In order not to be forgotten, he availed himself of another expedient: sending traditional gift packages to friends for the holidays: a habit that had never been interrupted, not even during the war and rationing. In order to get around the rationing regulations and the necessary coupons, he had to go around to pastry shops in different cities, especially Lindt in Zurich, Saipa in Lugano and Ravelli in Locarno, where he ended up from time to time.

Everyone who was anyone in Locarno went to the Caffè Ravelli in Piazza Grande, the main square where the International Film Festival with open-air showings is held every year. The café's regulars included town residents and celebrities:

Emil Ludwig, famous for a book on Mussolini; the writer Eric-Maria Remarque and the actress Paulette Goddard, Charlie Chaplin's ex-wife; the artists Jean Arp and Paul Klee; exiles like Egidio Reale and Ignazio Silone; the Aga Khan and Begum. Balzan always tried to impress, especially beautiful women, by sending them flowers and other delicacies. He made sure that the very beautiful Yvette Labrousse, the Begum, was among the recipients of his sumptuous gifts.

He also gave to charity and good causes incessantly: employees of the paper, charitable institutions, his home town of Badia Polesine, where he always sent gifts of assistance to the poor and donations to keep up his ties with the Veneto. But letters, acknowledgement from beneficiaries, visits – rarer because of the war that had closed the borders – were not enough to fill up Balzan's sense of solitude, nor was the theatre, music or invitations out and visits to people who had ties with Italy.

1943 was the crucial year: in Europe the situation was dramatic; Italy was laid waste. The radio and newspapers gave news of the Anglo-American bombings and German retreats. On 10 July the Allies landed in Sicily. In Switzerland, Balzan was always intent on his affairs, but not indifferent to the fate of his country. His apparently detached attitude suddenly changed after 25 July, as soon as Mussolini disappeared from the scene and the regime fell apart. Back from the Grisons, he telegraphed *Corriere* to have his mail sent directly to the Schweizerhof in Zurich. He hinted at a trip to Milan, and even called old friends on the phone. A brief period of euphoria followed, because the armistice had seemed to challenge everything.

Yet after the announcement of the armistice on 8 September 1943 and the events that followed, Balzan abandoned the idea of repatriating. The German occupation of Italy and the reappearance of Mussolini with the Social Republic forced thousands of political refugees to flee to Switzerland: among them were many figures from *Corriere*, and from circles he had

*Life in Switzerland*

known in Milan. They now came to him. While the drama of the nation was being acted out, Balzan in Zurich became a key figure in a discreet, but highly effective rescue mission. And so he again enshrouded himself in secrecy, and moved to the Hirslandenklinik in Witellikerstrasse 40, where he lived in seclusion. If he went out, it was mainly at night.

Why? Switzerland was full of refugees – military, Jewish, political – who were all asking for asylum. From Italy alone, over 40,000 were taken in. Among others, there were Luigi Einaudi, economist and later President of the Italian Republic in 1948, the industrialist and humanist from the Piedmont region Adriano Olivetti, Balzan's colleague Filippo Sacchi, the famous journalist Indro Montanelli, Mussolini's daughter Edda Ciano and Emilio Pucci, who became one of the most famous Italian designers after the war. There were also young people like Giorgio Strehler, future theatre director, film directors Luciano Emmer and Dino Risi, the tenor and friend of Maria Callas, Giuseppe Di Stefano. Finally, there were also turncoat Fascists like the comedy writer Sem Benelli and the industrialists Vittorio Cini and Giuseppe Volpi.

Balzan's gestures of solidarity were countless, without distinction in terms of old or new political militancy. Dino Alfieri, ex-ambassador to Berlin, one of the Fascist party officials who had voted against Mussolini on 25 July 1943 came to him immediately, and their relations remained confidential, even when the press campaigns against the presence of ex-party officials in Switzerland had started up.

A beneficiary was Claudio Soavi, his successor as manager, ousted in 1938 because he was Jewish. When he got to Lugano, he was recruited by Balzan, busy in his new role as grand patron of *Corriere* journalists. And so from January 1944 until his repatriation in May 1945, Soavi kept him up to date on new arrivals and prepared his press review, Balzan's mania. The different political groups had in fact obtained permission from the authorities to publish weekly sheets with Italian news in the Canton Ticino papers. Because of Swiss neutrality, the articles, written by the most famous antifascists on culture, politics and the economy, were published anonymously. Balzan's *factotum* Soavi selected articles, pseudonyms and writers he thought were worthy of his attention. From his reviews, we have a vivid portrait of that part of Italy in exile. Luigi Einaudi, a prestigious author of *Corriere* under the Albertini brothers, in Switzerland as a political refugee, even tried to get Balzan interested in the initiatives of the Liberal Party.

Another guest under Balzan's protection was Vittore Veneziani, director of the choir of La Scala in Milan, also in Switzerland for racial reasons. His friend took action to make it possible for him to keep up his musical career in Italian-speaking Switzerland: Veneziani was able to direct a local choir in the Italian Grisons and hold concerts with other internees. How did Balzan live in such a dramatic period, with arrivals, appeals, contradictory news? Above and beyond the assistance he gave with such well-aimed generosity, he did not allow intrusions into his private life. His stay at the Hirslanden clinic guaranteed him an orderly life that was sheltered from unforeseen developments. His days were all the same: a stop at the bank, avid reading of newspapers and letters, old and new friends from political exile, but they were always chosen, and to be seen only at his discretion.

The Marquis Rino De Nobili, diplomat in retirement in Ticino, at Villa Berra in Certenago (now the headquarters of The American School in Switzerland) and his wife Elsa Nathan-Berra were among the few who were close enough to him to be able to make him come out of his shell and confront reality anew. Their home became a meeting place for antifascists – Ferruccio Parri and Leo Valiani of the Committee of National Liberation passed through – and for Allied agents. Balzan, however, was not among this entourage, because in those

*Life in Switzerland*

months and for all of 1944 he stayed away from Lugano, which had become murkier than ever because of the spies and informers of all nationalities who were passing through.

Those who went to see him in Zurich were exiles who would not cause unpleasant surprises, like Giuseppe De Logu, former professor at the Accademia in Venice, a writer on art, and professor at the Italian Università Popolare (People's University) in Zurich. De Logu got him involved in a cultural initiative that caused a sensation. At the Kunsthaus in Zurich, an exhibition on his collection of nineteenth century Italian paintings (*Italienische Malerei des XIX. Jahrhunderts*) was held. The exhibition put his name back into circulation again after ten years of silence.

In the spring of 1945, the war came to an end and the clandestine counter-exodus from Switzerland to Italy – especially of politicians – began. Revenge came at the end of April: the insurrection of Milan, the flight of the Fascist party officials and neofascist supporters, the execution of Mussolini and his main collaborators – the Liberation, in short. This time the regime was truly finished. Balzan could go back to Italy, but instead, he stayed in Switzerland. Now that the Italian-Swiss border was hermetically closed on orders from the Allies, a commissioner of public safety acted as intermediary between Balzan and Milan from his office in Ponte Chiasso: the news Balzan received from this source persuaded him that it was not time to leave Switzerland yet.

CHAPTER SIX

# The Project

After the Liberation of Italy, Balzan could return to his country, but the situation seemed to be more confusing than ever. The news he received in Zurich was anything but reassuring: many of his colleagues had gone back to *Corriere*, but after the Liberation, others had to go into hiding because they were wanted for collaborationism. There was talk of arrest warrants, trials and summary executions. It was a time of reckoning, and so Balzan stayed in Switzerland.

He did not show up again in Milan until 1946, after thirteen years had gone by. In a certain sense, going back was a risk. On 11 May, the new La Scala theatre, which had been rebuilt after the bombings of August 1943, was inaugurated. It was the first festive occasion in the city after years of tragedy. Toscanini, Balzan's friend, had just come back from the United States, and conducted the performance. Balzan took his place in his box next to his old friends Sabatino Lopez, Arnaldo Fraccaroli, Renato Simoni and Arnaldo Sartori. The Crespi brothers were also there, thus filling out the ranks of the former *Corriere* staff.

The evening was crowded with "all of the civic authorities, the members of the Allied Commission, representatives of the foreign consulates", deputy prime minister Pietro Nenni and the ministers Carlo Sforza, Pierluigi Romita, Epicarmio Corbino, Giustino Arpesani and Mauro Scoccimarro. Among other politicians present were Riccardo Lombardi, Achille Marazza and Ferruccio Parri.

The new faces in politics were the anti-Fascists who had been in prison or in exile; among the older faces, many had prudently 'disappeared', because purges were still underway. Elections were just around the corner: two days earlier, Vittorio Emanuele III had abdicated, and the new king was Umberto II. The monarchy-republic referendum was set for 2 June 1946. The situation in Italy was still unstable: purges, tip-offs and vendettas continued in this time of reckoning, and someone could have tried to blow the whistle on Balzan for possible "collusion" with the Fascists, or attack him. Although he had shown signs of wanting to leave Switzerland for good, he went back immediately after the performance at La Scala and stayed in contact with his friends by mail.

He returned to Italy from time to time – once for a brief meeting on Lake Como with the owners of *Corriere,* who wanted him to take up his old post again at the paper's headquarters in Via Solferino. But the Crespi brothers had appointed a stalwart conservative, Guglielmo Emanuel, as new director. Since Balzan had known Emanuel for over fifty years, and was not at all well-disposed towards him, he refused to return to manage the *Corriere* firm as long as he was around. A long time passed before Balzan went back to Italy again after the war. With the way things were going, he shelved the idea of settling in Milan and made plans for his usual summer stint in Pontresina in Switzerland.

In the autumn, he went back to Zurich, where he received visitors with his usual discretion. The news that reached him from *Corriere* headquarters undoubtedly convinced him it was better to stay away from Italy, too. "If you only knew how badly off journalists in Milan are: it's better not to talk about it!...

## The Project

twelve new daily papers that only publish a heap of delusions and hare-brained ideas".

From Switzerland, he arranged for the usual works of charity in Italy and took care of business. In the private sphere, he kept up contacts with his long-standing friends. His base was still in Switzerland, with his usual comings and goings back and forth between Zurich, Lucerne and Lugano. After a great deal of hesitation, he decided to cross the Italian border again when the Christian Democrats won the elections of 1948 against the Communist and Socialist front. He had a new passport that had been issued by the Consulate General of Italy in Lugano. Moreover, it seems as though he had regained stability. He wanted to see his native Veneto region again, and went there with the two young Fisch brothers from Lugano, Ugo and Marco, who noted how deeply moved Balzan was when he saw the bust of his brother Luigi installed in the city hall of Badia Polesine when he returned to his native land after such a long absence. He may have been thinking of the commemoration ceremony in 1931.

With time, he found peace of mind and began to trust people again. So he made his address known and showed up in Milan, but he was always protected by a 'filter' of anonymity. In 1949 he began to make plans for going back to Italy definitively: declaring his fiscal position and gathering information about the new norms for foreigners entering and leaving Switzerland, and on residence permits in case he should want to return. When his residence permit expired in 1950 he left Zurich for good. He declared his legal residence in Badia, but his domicile was in Milan. He continued to go to the Canton Ticino as a tourist, staying at the Hotel Croce Bianca in Lugano.

Yet despite all these plans, he never stayed very long in any one place in Italy. He had people look for houses for him in Stresa, Sanremo or Venice, but he really spent his time travelling around. In the Veneto he had relatives, in Milan, colleagues, and around Lago Maggiore, friends – Toscanini lived there – but they were always well-chosen: "I can count my true friends on one hand," he said again and again. He was very demanding, and if someone disappointed him, there was no turning back.

Good health and successful business moves marked this period, which was on the whole positive. He watched his investments through a network of financial consultants, and his estate, which was already enormous, became even bigger. Payments, savings, pension – all were invested in industrial stocks (Nestlé) tied to the Swiss Franc. Thus, while the Italian Lira drastically fell in value because of the war and post-war inflation, his wealth was consolidated. It was a very intense period for him as a businessman, and his relations with the world of banking and finances paid off. He lived this phase of his life between Italy and Switzerland with his usual reserve, and during this time, his great financial skills gave rise to various myths about the origins of his capital, like the rumour that he had run off to Switzerland with the capital of the *Corriere* firm.

Everyone knew he was rich. Vincenzo Fagioli, an industrialist from Verona, wrote: "he had an exceptional sense of intuition for finances and business. It will suffice to say that when he died [...] he left 36 billion Lire." That was in 1953. However, Balzan's protégé Ugo Fisch, now one of Switzerland's most renowned otorhinolaryngologists, frequently went to see him in Lugano, remembers: "he talked about everything, but talking about money was taboo [...] you could tell that he had worked his way up, that he didn't look down on the world from his high horse. Of course he had a superior intellect, but above all he had the good sense to realize that worth was not just limited to money, because, in fact, he never talked about it."

Charity was a point of honour, and he set considerable amounts aside for the purpose. He took up contacts with Badia Polesine again in 1945, and in 1948 he sent a large sum to

## The Project

the city hall to be used for charity and for the city. After another act of solidarity with the poor of the town, he was made Honorary Chairman of the education trust. In Milan, he made donations to the Giuseppe Verdi home for retired musicians, and financed the journalists' club Il Circolo della Stampa with largesse so that he could share in the life of Milan's 'family' of the press. He also made hundreds of anonymous donations to private parties by means of discreet intermediaries. His generosity also extended to the Canton Ticino, where he kept informed about the needs of his fellow countrymen.

Balzan then turned his attention to his native Veneto region again when in 1951 a terrible flood submerged the Po River plain, causing him to relive the tragedy that had marked his adolescence. His visits to that unfortunate land steered him towards the idea of a "grandiose" project: "reconstructing the banks of the Po". But Fate had other plans.

Eugenio Balzan died of a heart attack in Lugano, on the evening of 15 July 1953. at the age of seventy-nine. Up to that day he had been strong and active; always attentive to his health. He had many projects, and obviously thought he would have time to carry them out. The following story is told by Balzan's long-time friend, the diplomat and journalist Cristano Ridòmi, in his collection of testimonials of those who were close to him in his final days.

As already mentioned, the whole Ridòmi family from Udine was very close to Balzan. Cristano's father Giuseppe had known Eugenio since the time of his military service, and both he and his brother had been watched over by Balzan at every stage of their careers, almost as if they were his sons. At the funeral in Lugano, Ridòmi contacted those present and wrote to his mother in Udine about the hours before Balzan's sudden death with the fondness of someone who was very dear to him. Ridòmi wrote that on 14 July: "Balzan did not feel well, and called his friends, the Fisch family, that morning saying that he wanted to go to the doctor's. He was diagnosed with a myocardial infarction that had probably been in course for some time. Fisch urged him to get someone to take him to the hospital in Moncucco. One of the maids he often liked to joke around with said that he had been pale for some time and hadn't even complained about the coffee being too weak or too strong. They put him to bed in the early afternoon, and perhaps because of the injections of sedatives, he fell asleep for a few hours. He had been examined by two physicians, both of whom did not try to conceal his desperate state. 'I was told to call Dr. Clemente Molo of Bellinzona, his friend', said the head of the Hotel Croce Bianca where he resided, 'when he arrived, he was already in death's throes, and could do no more than acknowledge that he was dead, in his room, no. 307, in my presence'."

The following day, Ridòmi wrote, "Eugenio held a rosary in his two large hands. We stood there for a while, then a few minutes outside. A truck with the coffin arrived, and in less than a quarter of an hour, it was closed and the zinc cover was welded shut. Then we went to the morgue and prayed next to Eugenio, while candles were lighted. No one else was there, neither family members nor friends – Fate had it that we would be the last ones to be near to him." Balzan's friend Arnaldo Sartori's thoughts were: "An end in solitude. For years I did everything humanly possible to convince him to change his way of life and to make him stop living like a vagrant. It hurt me to see him living with those three suitcases in that squalid little hotel room, and I had a premonition that it would end up like it did."

Many people knew he had a daughter, but no one had never seen her. Even those who were closest to the family were surprised to read that in Balzan's obituary, "his aggrieved daughter Lina announces the sad news". She was seen for the first time at the funeral in Lugano. And many also came to know – perhaps with surprise – that he also had two sisters, Edvige and Maria, with children and grandchildren.

## The Project

The funeral was widely publicised. *Corriere* published the obituary. Along with his daughter, the Crespis were also at the funeral. The director Mario Missiroli remembered him, as did his collaborators Claudio Soavi, Arnaldo Sartori, Arnaldo Fraccaroli and Orio Vergani. The writers Dino Buzzati, Arturo Lanocita, Francesco Pastonchi, Eligio Possenti and Carlo Zanicotti underlined his qualities of "character and great generosity" and his "big heart". Luigi Gasparotto, Arturo Toscanini and Vittore Veneziani remembered their long-lasting friendship, and Dino Alfieri recalled "his solidarity while in exile".

Among the many messages of sympathy, there was one from the head of the Italian government Luigi Einaudi, from the ambassador of Italy in Berne Egidio Reale and from the mayor of Badia. The mass was said at the church of the Sacro Cuore in Lugano, and at the cemetery there were Swiss and Italian authorities and colleagues. Gasparotto read the official salute. Ridòmi's account says, "at midday they slowly left the cemetery under a scorching sun." The coffin was immediately taken to Badia, where it was covered with funeral wreaths and other signs of condolences.

Ridòmi met Balzan's daughter Lina for the first time in Lugano, and his letter describes her as "a woman of about sixty, tall and distinguished," and he reports her first impressions about the death of her father: "I feel strange during this ceremony. Actually, among those present, I am the person who knew Eugenio Balzan least. If he had only known how dramatic my life has been." She was disoriented by what had happened and by the complications she had to face.

"A curious fate," Ridòmi comments. "Such an orderly, careful man apparently died without leaving a will. The authorities collected all of the things that were lying around in his room, and had the safe opened. There they found gold, stocks, etc., but no will." On the days before his death, Balzan had seemed to be worried. "I ran into him a few days before his death," recalls Ugo Fisch, "If I think about it [...] I was with my father in Piazza Riforma. Balzan said he had chest pains, and complained [...]When my father asked him, 'So why don't you go to the doctor's?' he said, 'I've got so many things that I want to finish before going to the doctor's. I have so many complicated things to straighten out." Fisch comments: "He wanted to do more for the country. He did not think he would die, and you can see that for good luck, he kept putting off the idea of having to make a will." What Balzan's 'great' project actually was is not clear, and it seems that he had not made a decision on any single idea. He may have had several things in mind. Ridòmi emphasizes that in "quiet, long-lasting work, in the areas that were close to him, Balzan found that his spirit and memory would be honoured. He was so unassuming, and wanted to preserve his anonymity in making his generous donations without ostentation or sensationalism [...] he often spoke of the hospitals in Milan and his hometown, Badia Polesine, of institutions for the poor and the elderly."

In his native Badia, people were certainly expecting a great bequest, and this is confirmed in the minutes of a city council meeting: "a few days before his death, he had proposed a visit to Badia, and hence to take an interest in its needs for the schools and in the possibility of starting up an industry in Badia". When the mayor went to visit him in Lugano, he learned of plans to restore – at his own expense – the town theatre where he had seen many performances as a youth.

Getting to work on these ideas meant, however, straightening out the fiscal problems connected with Swiss taxes and his residence permit, which Balzan had left hanging. Thus it was up to his daughter to deal with the pitfalls surrounding a legacy that according to great-grandnephew Riccardo Luzzatto "had been dumped on her, wreaking havoc on her life." In short, Lina Balzan Danieli suddenly found she had millions of Swiss francs in stocks and liquid assets. Up to that time, she had made her living by teaching French, and her father had always been there, with economic support, too.

Her mother was dead, and she already had that inheritance in Verona. Lina had suffered for years because her husband was far away, but had always admired her 'great daddy'. The enormous fortune that unexpectedly had come to her created a great deal of administrative difficulties because there were taxes to pay in Switzerland. The first to recommend caution was an old friend, Mario Mazzarotto, bank director of the Banca Nazionale del Lavoro: "think of the difficulties of succession, of all of those 'friends' who will now try to have their share of this inheritance. In the meanwhile, I'll give you this advice: don't sign anything, don't accept anything, many will want to take advantage of your weakness and lack of experience. So don't be in a hurry to do anything."

Since there was no will, the magistrate of Lugano appointed Lugano notary Pino Bernasconi administrator of the estate. From Balzan's very orderly inventory of his property, the estate was worth 31 million Swiss francs, and the amount was notified in all of the federal and cantonal authorities in Switzerland. The state council member and head of the Department of Finance in Ticino, Brenno Galli, was appointed receiver. On her part, Lina recognized the Canton Ticino's right "to investigate the extent of the capital" she had inherited.

They were months of anxiety because the "necessity" to move to the Swiss canton meant notifying the Swiss authorities of a change in residence, and that meant difficulties as far as exemption from "paying taxes in Italy" was concerned. Taxes, for that matter, involved everyone to a certain extent, even relatives. Despite her caution and search for trustworthy consultants, Lina was duped by a notary who charged her an astronomical fee for an unspecified transfer of funds in Liechtenstein. In any event, as heir, she paid all of the Swiss fiscal authorities – federal, cantonal and municipal – the required inheritance tax.

Lina continued her father's tradition of giving to charity with bequests in his memory. Ferruccio Lanfranchi, a famous writer for *Corriere*, got her involved in the creation of a clinic named after Balzan at the Association of Lombard Journalists in Milan. It was inaugurated in 1958 by the President of the Italian Republic Gronchi, and could take care of up to 4,500 patients in 1964.

The first initiatives, however, were financed by Lina in Switzerland. The most significant came at the end of 1953 on the advice of Arturo Lang, bank director and long-standing friend and financial consultant of her father: a donation to build a school to help handicapped children, the OTAF in Lugano-Sorengo, with its Eugenio Balzan Pavillion that was inaugurated in 1955.

But the name of Lina Balzan is mainly linked to the Foundation that was also dedicated to Eugenio Balzan for a long-term project. The idea for a foundation came to the women of the Balzan family, and in particular to Paola Pilogallo, Eugenio's sister Maria's daughter. A refined, learned woman with many interests, she convinced Lina to link the name of her father to a 'grand scale' institution of international renown.

Lina approved the rules and regulations of the future International Balzan Foundation in 1956. However, amidst the many relatives and disinterested friends who helped her, she ran up against people who were in part bunglers and in part swindlers in this case, too. Although ill, she was persuaded to take a tour of America, New York and Venezuela, to see to certain investments. She came back very weak. On 2 June, she signed her will, which she left in Switzerland with the notary Franco Maspoli.

On 15 June 1956 in Lugano the International Balzan Foundation was created with the aim of "fostering culture, the sciences and the most meritorious humanitarian initiatives of peace and brotherhood among peoples, regardless of nation-

*The Project*

ality, race or creed by assigning three different prizes: 1. for peace, humanity and brotherhood among peoples; 2. for literature, the moral sciences and the arts; 3. for the physical, mathematical and natural sciences and medicine."

Lina entered the San Rocco clinic in Lugano, then went to the hospital of Sant'Anna, and then went back to Milan, although "in great pain". She spent some time in Nervi, near Genoa on the Ligurian coast, in the hopes that the mild climate would help her recover. On 3 February 1957, the Foundation was officially constituted; on 28 February she signed the acts and the rules and regulations. On the night of 1 March 1957, Angela Lina Balzan died in Milan.

CHAPTER SEVEN

# The Painting Collection

Among the luxuries that Balzan allowed himself was a collection of nineteenth century Italian paintings, which he started between 1910 and 1920 in emulation of the collectors from the *Corriere* milieu, the Albertini and the Crespi families. They contributed to developing a mature taste for art in the young Balzan.

His contacts with a varied intellectual world, with dealers and art critics guided him in purchases of canvases by painters of every region in Italy from the end of the nineteenth to the beginning of the twentieth century. The works in the Balzan collection are from the period beginning in 1860, which, to use the words of the contemporary Neapolitan philosopher and historian Benedetto Croce, can be described as "the unity of the history of Italy," and the only period that truly counts for Italian painting of the nineteenth century, both because it marks a renewal, and because of the intrinsic moral and patriotic values that it expresses.

Balzan's tastes in collecting are typical of the upper classes in Lombardy at the time, with preferences for Risorgimento values and themes. The collection has a unity of aesthetic expression with an 'atmosphere' of its own, which could also be a reflection of his family's patriotism. Of course, it undeniably shows how wealthy he was, because Balzan now had the means to hobnob with gallery owners and art experts who advised him in purchasing pieces and considered him as a 'serious collector'.

The one who influenced him most was Oreste Silvestri, whom he became very close to. Son of the painter Carlo Silvestri, a patriot of The Five Days of Milan (1848), Oreste attended the Accademia di Brera, and was among the last students of Francesco Hayez – the friend of painter Giovanni Segantini – and made a name for himself through his atelier in the centre of Milan in the Galleria Vittorio Emanuele and as a restorer of antique paintings. He was called upon to do restoration work on Leonardo da Vinci's *Last Supper* in the church of Santa Maria delle Grazie, and in 1924 was nominated head conservator of the painting.

Oreste's artistic ideals were similar to Balzan's, and were influenced by collectors like his friend the industrialist Gino Bassi (with whom he was almost in competition for the best pieces). Balzan took Silvestri's advice in buying paintings. Created through accurate research, the collection unites artists of the last regional schools of Italy, from the Piedmont to Naples, from Lombardy to Lazio and from the Veneto to Apulia. Among Lombard artists are Leonardo Bazzaro of the naturalist school, and Eugene Gignous, whose preferred subjects are landscapes from the Lago Maggiore region. Other painters include Domenico Induno, Hayez's friend, who paints subjects that range from historical subjects to the emotions and daily life of the poor. Another great artist in the collection is the great *vedutista* and portrait painter Mosé Bianchi, who took part in exhibitions all over Europe with views of Milan and the Venetian lagoon. Another landscapist, Emilio Praga, is also represented, with his views of Lombardy.

The collection also includes works by artists from the Venetian schools, like Achille Beltrame from Vicenza, who painted historical subjects and cityscapes. He was the illustrator of *Corriere's* innovative weekly magazine *Domenica del Corriere*

## The Painting Collection

– Balzan's creation – and its great success was largely due to his drawings of current events. Other painters from the Veneto are Giacomo Favretto, with scenes set in the eighteenth century, and Luigi Nono, with his landscapes and intimate scenes.

There are also works by Abruzzese artists, like Paolo Michetti, illustrator of Gabriele D'Annunzio's works. His pastels and works in tempera of the Verist school were exhibited in all of the major European capitals. Filippo Palizzi is another Verist painter from Abruzzo, and his speciality was animal scenes. To complete the collection are artists from other regions of Italy. Gaetano Previati was from Ferrara, Antonio Fontanesi from Reggio Emilia; Ardengo Soffici from Florence painted in a style similar to the French Impressionists. Giovanni Fattori, from Livorno, painted landscapes and military subjects. The Neapolitan school is represented by Domenico Morelli, with his romantic re-evocations of historical and exotic scenes, and Giuseppe De Nittis, who was also active in Paris and London, with studies of Vesuvius. Thus the collection reflects a certain kind of taste in the history of early twentieth century collecting - experimental currents were not part of Balzan's world.

He took a distance from the collection when he moved to Switzerland in 1933. For ten years the paintings remained in Milan, where he kept his official residence. Then, surprisingly, they appeared at the Kunsthaus in Zurich, when on 5 April 1944, the exhibition *Italienische Malerei des XIX. Jahrhunderts* opened. It was Balzan's collection, replete with a catalogue with a preface by the art critic Giuseppe De Logu, in exile in Zurich since the end of the 1930s.

The Swiss press gave a great deal of coverage to the show. It travelled to the Italian part of Switzerland, to Bellinzona, and the number of works exhibited doubled as works from private Swiss and Italian collections, including Toscanini's, were shown along with Balzan's. It then went on to the Kunstmuseum in Berne. The catalogue, which Balzan undoubtedly had the idea for and hence financed, was sent to numerous refugees. In the capital of the Canton Ticino, the exhibit had a much greater symbolic significance than in Zurich, because the proceeds from catalogue sales went to the Red Cross for Italian exiles, and because the initiative was understood as a way to strengthen ties between Switzerland and Italy.

Why did Balzan embark on this project in the middle of the Second World War? We can find out something about the background leading up to the exhibition from the letters of Attilio Tamaro, former Minister of Italy in Berne, who in the 1950s reconstructed the *iter* of the collection. He ordered its importation to the Italian legation in Berne – hence legally in Italian territory – so that when Balzan gave the word after the war was over, it would go back to Italy.

In June 1943, Tamaro was replaced by Massimo Magistrati, the brother-in-law of Mussolini's daughter Edda Ciano. Balzan thus lost a precious foothold, since Tamaro was the key figure in the "painting operation". With the exhibit in Zurich, Balzan wanted to make his ownership of the paintings known, while at the same time justifying the presence of the collection in Switzerland and earning the praise of the Swiss authorities for his charitable aims in favour of war refugees.

Years later, in 1950, when Balzan was officially back in Italy, the collection turned up again at the Accademia di Belle Arti di Venezia after 1950. How had he managed to bring the collection back into the country? Once he had decided to buy a house in Venice, Balzan made sure that his friend De Logu – who had gone back to his post as director of the Accademia di Belle Arti – made the paintings reach him with a "temporary import permit", which could be renewed periodically. When Balzan died in 1953, his daughter and heir, Angela Lina, managed to settle customs complications and keep the paintings in Italy. The collection now adorns the rooms of the Balzan Prize Foundation headquarters in Milan.

# APPENDICES

# Chronology

1874. Eugenio Amedeo Francesco Balzan is born in Badia Polesine (Rovigo) on 20 April, to Angelina Bonato and Lorenzo Balzan, landowner.

1881. The family moves to Padua, where Eugenio could go to school.

1882. The Adige River bursts its banks and wipes out the Balzan family's property in Masi.

1883. The family goes to Valli Mocenighe, where the father has a position as land agent for Count Mocenigo.

1884. Eugenio starts work in a ceramics factory.

1886. Attends artisans' school for two years in Padua.

1888. The family moves back to Padua.

1889. Balzan works as a decorator in Padua and Abano, then moves in with his Aunt Luisa Balzan in Verona.

1890. Studies with a tutor in order to embark on a military career.

1891. His aunt Luisa Balzan pays for his enrolment in the Military Academy in Modena.

1892. Eugenio marries Itala Bella Maria Adami of Verona, in a church wedding in Padua. Takes a job in Milan. Their daughter Angela Luigia Maria, or Lina for short, is born. Returns to Verona. His brother Paolo dies.

1893. Does military service in the Savoy Cavalry. His brother Luigi dies.

1894. Accepted at the technical institute for surveyors in Mantua, and starts working at the cadastre in Verona.

1895. Attends night courses in Verona at the Istituto Sant'Eufemia.

1896. Attends night courses for city clerks in Mantua, works for a surveying firm in Verona, and takes his diploma in surveying at Turin. His sister Lavinia dies.

1897. Holds position as surveyor in Vicenza, and begins writing stories for the newspaper *L'Arena* in Verona. Gets a job as proof-reader at *Corriere della Sera* in Milan.

1898. Promoted to reporter, then head reporter. His father Lorenzo dies.

1899. Correspondent for *Il Secolo XIX* and for *La Gazzetta di Venezia*.

*Chronology*

1900. Correspondent for *Il Giornale di Sicilia* and *Il Pungolo* of Naples.

1901. Special envoy to Canada for an investigative report on Italian emigrants.

1902. Special envoy to Switzerland.

1903. Nominated managing director of the publishing firm of *Corriere della Sera*.

1905. Nominated arbitrator for grievances with foreign countries.

1906. Starts illustrated supplements to *Corriere*.

1907. Through his initiative *Corriere* becomes owner of *Guerin Meschino*.

1908. Travels to St. Petersburg on private matters for the Albertini family.

1910. Marriage to Itala Adami annulled. Is knighted.

1911. Named officer to the crown.

1912. Promoted to *commendatore*, and nominated chairman of the union of newspaper editors.

1914. Diploma of participation in the book and graphic arts fair in Leipzig.

1917. Exonerated from the call to arms.

1918. Appointed to handle legal matters for the *Corriere* firm.

1921. President of the Federation of Italian Editors. His mother dies.

1922. Is approached by Mussolini, who wants to know what the owners of *Corriere* think of the March on Rome.

1923. Mediator between Luigi Albertini and the Crespi brothers in the buy out of *Corriere*.

1924. Telegrams to Mussolini to prevent boycotting of *Corriere*. Resigns as President of the Federation of Italian Editors (FIEG). Attacked in the Galleria Vittorio Emanuele in Milan by Fascist squads.

1925. Intermediary between the Albertini and the Crespi families, becomes shareholder of *Corriere* with one quota. Flanks the new director Pietro Croci, and is slandered for presumed "offence against the head of the government."

1926. Flanks new director Ugo Ojetti.

1927. Acquisition of *Il Secolo*, saves antifascist journalists who left *Corriere* or who were threatened with getting the sack.

1928. Flanks new director Maffio Maffii.

1929. Flanks new director Aldo Borelli.

1930. Augusto Turati, secretary of the Fascist party and his supporter, is dismissed.

1931. Participates in the commemoration ceremonies for his

brother Luigi in Badia Polesine, and institutes a scholarship in his name. Sudden death of Arnaldo Mussolini, brother of the Duce and friend to Balzan.

1932. Gold medal of merit from the association of newspaper editors. Is reported to the secret police OVRA by an informer.

1933. Handles legal matters for the Crespi brothers. Moves to Switzerland for health reasons, but does not go back to *Corriere*.

1934. Upon his 60th birthday, receives his severance pay and moves to Zurich, with stays in Lugano.

1936. Watched by the Italian political police in the Canton Ticino.

1938. Watched by the Swiss police because of a kidnapping attempt.

1939. Stays in Zurich, Lucerne and Lugano. Submits paperwork to obtain Swiss citizenship.

1943. Fascism falls and Balzan is about to repatriate, but at the armistice he goes back to Zurich, as guarantor for Italian political refugees, especially journalists of *Corriere della Sera*.

1944. Undertakes an exhibition of his painting collection in Zurich and Bellinzona.

1945. At the end of the war, remains in Switzerland.

1946. Goes back to Milan for the reopening of the Scala, with his friend Arturo Toscanini conducting. Turns down job as director of *Corriere d'Informazione*.

1947. Stays in Zurich, Pontresina, Lucerne and Lugano, seeing to his estate.

1948. Renews his passport and travels to the Veneto.

1949. Stays in Zurich and Lugano, and distinguishes himself for charitable work to Italian institutions.

1950. Transfers his residence to Badia Polesine. Visits to the Canton Ticino as tourist.

1951. After the flooding of the Po/Adige river plain, makes plans to improve the region.

1953. Dies on 15 July in Lugano, where the funeral takes place. The body is buried in Badia. His daughter Lina Balzan Danieli inherits a considerable estate and entertains the idea of a cultural foundation.

1956. Lina underwrites the rules and regulations of the nascent International Balzan Foundation.

1957. Rules and regulations of the International Balzan Foundation signed, and constituted with the estate inherited from her father. Lina Balzan dies in Milan on 1 March.

# Biographical Sketches

ALBERTINI, ALBERTO (b. Ancona 1879 – d. Naples 1954) Journaist and writer. At *Corriere della Sera* in 1899, and officially director from 1921-25, when his brother Luigi took up politics, although for all practical purposes director since 1914. Spent the last years of his life in Capri, where he wrote religious meditations.

ALBERTINI, LUIGI (b. Ancona 1879 – d. Rome 1941) Journalist and politician. Among the most influential of the liberal elite of pre-Fascist Italy. After his university degree in law, joined *Corriere della Sera* in 1896, becoming director and co-owner in 1900. Nominated senator in 1914, and ousted as owner of *Corriere* in 1925 by Mussolini because of his opposition to Fascism. Retired in Torreimpietra (Rome), where he wrote historiographical works.

ALEARDI GAETANO «ALEARDO» (b. Verona 1812 – d. Verona 1978) Risorgimento patriot and politician. Participated in anti-Austrian movements in the Veneto in 1848-49 with Niccolò Tommaseo and Daniele Manin. Imprisoned in 1852 and 1859, and after the Unity of Italy elected member of Parliament, then appointed senator. Professor of aesthetics at the Accademia di Belle Arti in Florence.

ALFIERI, DINO [ODOARDO] (b. Bologna 1886 – d. Rome 1966) Party official and diplomat. Under-secretary of Corporations in 1929, Under-Secretary of the Press and Propaganda in 1935, Minister of Popular Culture in 1936, Ambassador to the Holy See in 1939, and in Berlin after 1940. After elections on 25 July 1943 against Mussolini, fled to Switzerland on 24 October. Condemned to death by the Fascist courts in Verona on 10 January 1944, but exonerated by the Purge Committee in 1946 and returned to Italy in 1948.

AYMO, GIOVANNI ANTONIO (b. Varallo Sesia 1861 – d. Bologna 1901). Journalist. After studies in chemistry became an assistant in a pharmacy. Began to write for newspapers in the Piedmont, then emigrated to Mexico, where he founded *Il Corriere Universale*, the first local Italian newspaper. Director of *L'Arena* of Verona, and co-owner since 1894.

BARZINI, LUIGI, senior (b. Orvieto 1874 – d. Milan 1947). Journalist. Joined *Corriere della Sera* in 1900. Went first to London, then was war correspondent in China and in the conflict between Japan and the Russian empire in 1904-05. Took part in the Peking-Paris motor rally in 1907, and was correspondent for the war between Italy and Turkey in 1911. In WWI, he supported the irredentism of Fiume and Dalmatia. In 1923, he founded *Corriere d'America* in Dallas, Texas (USA), but when the paper went bankrupt, he returned to Italy and became special envoy to *Il Popolo d'Italia*, then director of *Il Mattino di Napoli* in 1932 and was appointed senator in 1934. He supported the Italian Social Republic (Repubblica sociale italiana or RSI) and from October 1943 to April 1945 directed the official news agency Stefani-Morgagni. His wife Mantica Pesavento (d. 1941) was from the Veneto. After taking a degree in the hu-

manities at the Sorbonne, became a fiction writer. His son
Ettore, whom Balzan was godfather to, died in the concentration camp in Dachau in 1944.

BORELLI, ALDO (b. Vibo Valentia 1890 – d. Rome 1965).
Journalist. Hired by the Stefani agency, political correspondent in Rome for the newspaper *Il Mattino* in 1912, director of *La Nazione di Firenze* in 1915, correspondent from the front in WWI. Became member of the Fascist National Party (Partito nazionale fascista or PNF) in 1922, and secretary of the Fascist union of journalists in Tuscany. Director of *Corriere della Sera* from 1929 to 26 July 1943. In eastern Africa in 1935-36. In 1950 became head of the Roman edition of *L'Epoca*, and and in 1952, president of the editorial group Il *Giornale d'Italia*, and held these positions until his death.

BORLETTI, SENATORE (b. Milan 1880 – d. Milan 1939) Industrialist. In 1917 bought out the Alle Cento Città d'Italia warehouses of Fernando Bocconi and founded the department store La Rinascente. Friend of D'Annunzio, he financed his march on Fiume in 1919. Vice-president of the Banca Nazionale di Credito in 1928, president of the institution for disabled servicemen, and councillor for the Ente Autonomo della Scala. Senator from 1929 onwards, and was made Count of Arosio in 1937.

BORSA, Mario (b. Somaglia 1870 – d. Milan 1952) Journalist and literary critic. Worked for the newspaper *La Perseveranza*, and after 1896, for *Il Secolo*, which sent him to London, where he remained for fifteen years as a writer for the *The Daily News*. Was also a correspondent from Milan for *The Times* for forty years. Editor-in-chief of *Il Secolo* after WWI, but left the paper in 1923. Expelled from the union of journalists, then called by the Albertinis to write unsigned editorials on foreign policy for *Corriere della Sera*. In 1935 imprisoned for his anti-Fascism, and sanctioned in 1936. After the victory of the republic in 1946, he was fired by the Crespis because of the democratic line that characterised the newspaper, and was replaced.

BUZZATI, DINO (b. Belluno 1906 – d. Milan 1972) Journalist and writer. At *Corriere della Sera* in 1928 as reporter, after 1929 assistant music critic and head editor of supplements *La Lettura* and *La Domenica del Corriere*. In 1933 became famous with the novel *Bernabò delle montagne* (Barnabo of the Mountains) and took over the cultural page of *Corriere*. Special envoy after 1936, and war correspondent after 1940. Also a painter and novelist; he won the prestigious Strega literary prize in 1958.

CAMPIGLI, MASSIMO [MAX IHLENFELD] (b. Berlin 1895 – d. Saint Tropez 1971) Journalist and painter. Secretary to Renato Simoni for the literary supplement *La Lettura* from 1914. Volunteer in WWI, was captured and taken prisoner in Germany, then deported to Hungary in 1916. Escaped to Russia, then went back to Italy and became a correspondent for *Corriere della Sera* from Paris in 1919, where he took up painting, and exhibited his works in Rome in 1923. Became one of the Seven Italians of Paris in 1926, and left journalism in 1927. Post-cubist and Purist, he was invited to take part in the Venice Biennale of 1928, and became famous throughout Europe. Did part of the decoration of the Triennale in Milan in 1933 and the League of Nations in Geneva in 1937.

CIVININI, GUELFO (b. Livorno 1873 – d. Rome 1954) Journalist and novelist. Collaborated with *Il Giornale d'Italia*, and was special envoy for *Corriere della Sera* after 1907. Wrote on the Italian-Turkish war of 1911, Serbo-Turkish war of 1912 and WWI. Crepuscular and D'Annunzian poet, won the Viareggio Prize in 1937. Member of the Academy of Italy and Consul General to Calcutta in 1939.

CRESPI, ALDO (b. Milan 1885 – d. Merate 1978) Industrialist. Heir to manufacturing firms, agricultural and electrical companies, and co-owner of *Corriere della Sera*. Married Giuseppina Fossati Bellani. His daughter Giulia Maria Mozzoni Crespi is now president of FAI, an organization to preserve Italian cultural and artistic heritage. Knighted in 1964. Collector of antique silver and paintings.

D'ANNUNZIO, GABRIELE (b. Pescara 1863 – d. Gardone Riviera 1938) Writer, playwright and poet. In 1881, moved to Rome, where he took up journalism, then to Naples. Once back in Abruzzo, published works in prose, and through his relationship with the actress Eleonora Duse, began intense theatre production. Member of Parliament in 1897. After a period in France, where he was part of the high society of the *belle époque* and wrote for *Corriere della Sera*, he returned to Italy in 1915 and, supporting interventionism, took part in WWI. Deemed a national hero, he led the battle for the annexation of Istria and Dalmatia with the march on Fiume, setting up the Italian Regency of Carnaro, which fell in 1920. Retired to Gardone. Honoured by the Fascist regime, but lived a solitary life until his unexpected death.

DE NOBILI, RINO (b. La Spezia 1889 – d. Lugano 1947), Diplomat and Marquis of Vezzano. From a family with strong Risorgimento traditions, in 1912 attaché to Legation in Vienna and then in Berlin, member of Parliament in the XXVII legislature. In 1826 left politics and with his wife Elsa Nathan Berra, retired in Certenago di Montagnola, near Lugano (Switzerland). During WWII, their home, Villa Berra, became a meeting point for anti-Fascists and Allied agents. After the war, De Nobili was Ambassador in Brussels.

EINAUDI, LUIGI (b. Carrù 1874 – d. Rome 1961) Economist, journalist and politician. Secretary to the editor and then director of the famous review *Riforma Sociale* (Social Reform). Worked for *La Stampa*, then from 1900 to 1925 at *Corriere della Sera* – which he left together with the Albertinis – as commentator on economic and financial policy. Senator in 1919, university professor, rector of the University of Turin in September 1943. Expatriated to Switzerland and repatriated in December 1944 at the request of the government in Rome. Governor of the Bank of Italy from 1945 onwards, and was also member of the Constitutional Court, member of the Constituent Assembly in 1946 and Minister of the Budget in 1947. President of the Republic in 1948, and made senator for life in 1955.

FAGIUOLI, VINCENZO (b. Verona 1894 – d. Rome 1985) Industrialist. Volunteer in WWI. Enrolled in the Fascist National Party (PNF) in 1920, took part in the March on Rome, and was one of the secretaries for the Minister of Finance De Stefani from 1922 to 1925. Sent to Africa by the Institute for Industrial Reconstruction (IRI), and made Grand Officer of the Crown in 1929. President of the Italian Society for Foreign Commerce (SICE), and after 1937 coordinated the exportation of war materials to help Franco in Spain. In 1939 sent by Ciano to negotiate Italian neutrality with the French in Egypt, but fell into disfavour in 1943. Head of the Service for Civil and Economic Affairs in Athens, supported the Italian Social Republic (RSI), and held the post from October to December 1943. Repatriated in

*Biographical Sketches*

March 1944. After the war, was sent by Minister Carlo Sforza to retrieve Italian property in Egypt.

FARINACCI, ROBERTO (b. Isernia 1892 – d. Vimercate 1945) Journalist and lawyer. Volunteer in WWI. Founded the newspaper *Cremona nuova* – then *Regime fascista*. Member of a Fascist squad, provincial party secretary for Cremona from 1921 to 1929, member of the Great Council from 1923 to 1929 and from 1935 to 1943, secretary of the party from 1925 to 1926, member of Parliament after 1924, national councillor after 1939, Minister of State after 1938. After 25 July 1943, fled to Germany, where he led the first Fascists. Supporter of the RSI, he was arrested in Lecco, and shot on 28 April 1945.

FISCH, FEDERICO (b. Lugano 1892 – d. Lugano 1955) Swiss dentist and philanthropist. Studied at Zurich, graduating in odontoiatry. Opened a people's clinic and dentistry service in the schools in Canton Ticino. On the Commission for musical programmes for the Italian Swiss Radio, president of the Swiss Alpine Club, and founding member and chairman of the Odontological Society and the Natural Sciences Society in Ticino. On the Board of Directors for the Melisa - Messaggerie bookstores in Lugano.

GASPAROTTO, LUIGI (b. Sacile 1873 – d. Roccolo di Cantello 1954) Lawyer and politician. Member of Parliament from 1913 to 1929, Vice-president of the House in 1921, Minister of War in 1921-22. After 8 September 1943 political exile in Switzerland. Repatriated to Rome in 1944. After the war, was Minister of Aeronautics and Post-War Assistance. Member of the Constitutional Court in 1945, Member of the Constituent Assembly in 1946, Minister of Defence in 1947. Senator and President of the Trade Fair of Milan.

HOEPLI, ULRICO (b. Tuttwil 1847 – d. Milan 1935) Swiss publisher and bookseller. Trained in Zurich from 1862 to 1866, and then in Mainz, Trieste and Morgenstern in Breslau until 1870. Invited to Cairo in 1868-69 by Ismail Pascià, Khedive of Egypt, with the task of reorganizing the library, he then moved to Milan in 1870, and bought a bookstore. Started printing his own popular small-format technical and scientific manuals written in a clear writing style that guaranteed success. Also printed various series and limited editions, including Leonardo da Vinci's *Codex Atlanticus*, the *Codex Virgilianus* with annotations by Petrarch, and then Mussolini's *Opera Omnia* after 1933. He also created a section of rare books in his book store and donated the Zeiss Planetarium to the city of Milan in 1930.

LANFRANCHI, FERRUCCIO (b. Milan 1903 – d. Milan 1973) Journalist. Worked on news coverage at *Corriere della Sera* from 1924 onwards. Not enrolled in the Fascist union of journalists, and banished in 1928. In July of 1943, published various behind-the-scenes stories in *Corriere* on Fascist doings and had to seek refuge in Switzerland in March 1944, where he edited the column for the free zone of Ossola in the newssheet of the Christian Democrats in exile. After the war, head editor at *Corriere della Sera* until 1968. Supporter of the Eugenio Balzan Clinic for journalists. Author of books on the history of the Resistance.

LUZZATTO, RICCARDO (b. Milan 1935). Grand-nephew of Eugenio Balzan. Lawyer and professor of international law at the Università degli Studi di Milano.

MAFFII, MAFFIO (b. Florence 1881 – d. Rome 1957) Journalist. Correspondent from Florence for *Il Mattino* in 1904, directror of *Il Giornale di Vicenza* after 1908, and head edi-

*Biographical Sketches*

tor of *La Tribuna* of Treviso in 1940. Head of Mussolini's press office in 1924-25, director of *Corriere della Sera* from 1927 to 1929, and director of *La Nazione* of Florence from 1932 to 25 July 1943. Put on trial for his activities during the Fascist period, but was exonerated in 1948.

MALAPARTE, CURZIO [KURT SUCCKERT] (b. Prato 1898 – d. Rome 1957). Journalist and writer. Republican union official, volunteer in WWI and took part in Mussolini's March on Rome. Director of *La Stampa* in 1930, and dismissed in 1931. Sentenced to five years' enforced residence in Forte dei Marmi for his book *Technique du coup d'etat* (The Technique of Revolution). Worked for *Corriere della Sera* between 1932 and 1943. War correspondent on the Russian front from 1941-42, then liason officer with the Allies in liberated Italy in 1944. After the war, enrolled in the Italian Communist Party, and in his will, left his villa on Capri to China.

MAPELLI, MARIO (b. Milan 1907 – d. Milan 1984) Accountant. After taking a diploma in economic studies at the Bocconi University, became general accountant at *Corriere della Sera* (1933). Expelled from the paper for a short time in May 1945, but was immediately readmitted. Managing director until 1970.

MONDADORI, ARNOLDO (b. Poggio Rusco 1889 – d. Milan 1971) Publisher. Among the writers for the periodical *Luce!* in 1907, opened printing shops in Ostiglia and then moved them to Verona in 1917. Founder and president of the Mondadori publishing firm and of the executive committee of periodicals of the Italian Federation of Newspaper Publishers in Milan in 1921. Expatriated to Switzerland in November 1943, and prepared to restructure the firm in Lugano. Repatriated in June 1945. Received a gold medal for publishing in 1955, and the Libro d'oro book prize in 1958.

MONELLI, PAOLO (b. Fiorano Modenese 1891 – d. Rome 1984) Journalist and writer. Took part in WWI. Writer and correspondent for various Italian newspapers. Joined *Corriere* in 1926, and at the fall of Fascism, returned to *La Stampa* from 1946 to 1967.

MONTANELLI, INDRO (b. Fucecchio 1909 – d. Milan 2001) Journalist and writer. In 1934 with *Il Popolo d'Italia*, and in 1936 volunteer in eastern Africa. Correspondent for *Il Messaggero* in Spain in 1937, expelled from the Fascist National Party (PNF) and struck off the professional register, he was director of the Italian Institute of culture in Tallin, Estonia, then envoy for *Corriere della Sera* after 1941. After 25 July 1943 took risks, and was arrested and imprisoned, then expatriated to Switzerland, where he lived, back and forth between Lugano and Davos. In 1946 director of the illustrated weekly *La Domenica degli Italiani*, then special envoy for *Corriere della Sera*. Founded *Il Giornale Nuovo* in 1974, and *La Voce* in 1994, then went back to *Corriere*. Author of "popular history" books.

MUSSOLINI, ARNALDO (b. Dovia di Predappio 1885 – d. Milan 1931) Journalist and diplomat. Surveyor and teacher, he resided for a short time in Berne in 1904. Town Clerk in the Veneto, fought on the Piave River after Caporetto (1917). Managing director (including politics) from 1922 onwards of *Il Popolo d'Italia*. Headmaster of the Province of Forlì, president of the advisory committee for the national service for reforestation of the mountainous areas. Granted an honorary degree in agricultural science from the Università degli Studi di Milano.

*Biographical Sketches*

MUSSOLINI, BENITO (b. Dovia di Predappio 1883 – d. Giulino di Mezzegra 1945) Journalist and politician. Director of *L'Avvenire del lavoratore* in Trento from 1909 onwards, and secretary of the Socialist Party in Forlì after 1910. Director of *Avanti!* from 1912 onwards. Founded and was director of *Il Popolo d'Italia*. After 1914, interventionist. Took part in WWI. Creator of the *Fasci di combattimento* movement in 1919, and founder of the Fascist National Party (PNF) and member of Parliament in 1921. Head of the government from 29 October 1922 until 25 July 1943, and commander of the Miltia after 1926. First Marshal of the Empire from 1938 onwards, and Supreme Commander of the armed forces after 1940. Arrested on 25 July 1943, and freed by the Germans on 12 September. Founded the Republican Fascist Party (PFR), became head of state and of the Fascist Republican government after 23 September, and of the Italian Social Republic from 1 December 1943 to 27 April 1945. Captured by the partisans and shot on 28 April 1945.

NOBILE, UMBERTO (b. Lauro 1885 – d. Rome 1978) Explorer and Officer in the Genio Aeronautico division of the air force. Specialist in the study and construction of dirigibles. Upon commission from the Norwegian Aeroclub, built the Norge in Italy, and took part in the Amundsen-Ellsworth polar expedition in 1926. After the failure and controversy over the voyage of the "Italia" in 1928, resigned from the air force and moved to the Soviet Union from 1932 to 1936, and to the United States from 1939 1942. Reintegrated after the liberation in 1945, and member of the Constituent Assembly. Wrote books of memoirs.

OJETTI, UGO (b. Rome 1871 – d. Florence 1946) Journalist and writer. Graduated in law. Collaborated with different journals in Florence. In 1894 with *Il Giornale d'Italia* and in 1898 with *Corriere della Sera*, which he became director of from 1925 to 1927. Founded journals on art and literature: *Dedalo* in 1920, *Pegaso* in 1922 and *Pan* in 1933. Member of the Academy of Italy in 1930. On the executive committee of the *Enciclopedia italiana*. During the RSI, vice-president of the Academy of Italy from 1944 to April 1945.

PUCCINI, GIACOMO (b. Lucca 1858 – d. Brussels 1924) Composer. Attended the Istituto Musicale in Lucca and the Conservatory in Milan. Famous for the operas *Manon Lescaut* (1893), *La Bohème* (1886), *Tosca* (1900), *Madama Butterfly* (1904), *La fanciulla del West* (1910), *La Rondine* (1917), *Gianni Schicchi* (1918) and the incomplete *Turandot*, which was performed posthumously in 1926 at the Scala.

RIDÒMI, CRISTANO (b. Udine 1904 – d. Gardone Riviera 1969) Journalist. Government official and correspondent for *Corriere della Sera* from Berlin in 1930, in China and Manciukuò in 1937. Press agent for the Italian Embassy in Vienna in 1937, and Berlin in 1938. Head of the press office for the Prime Ministry in 1949. Writer for *Il Popolo* from 1951 to 1954, then president of the Italian television network RAI.

RIDÒMI, GIUSEPPE (b. Udine 1874 – d. Udine 1939) Tradesman. President of the Tradesmen's Union in Friuli from 1903 onwards, then secretary and president of the Federation of Tradesmen and Shopkeepers in the Region.

ROSSI, ADOLFO (b. Fratta Polesine 1857 – d. Buenos Aires 1921) Journalist and diplomat. Travelled throughout the

Americas and Africa, where he wrote his first journalistic pieces. Published *Un italiano in America* (An Italian in America) in 1891. At *Corriere della Sera* from 1895 onwards, and head editor in 1897. An adventurous individual, expert on military matters and first permanent war correspondent at *Corriere*. In Eritrea for the campaign of 1895, in Greece for the conflict with Turkey in 1896 and in Spain in 1898 for the war with the United States. Left *Corriere* in 1901 to enter the commission on emigration and started a consular career in Argentina.

SACCHI, FILIPPO (b. Vicenza 1887 – d. Pietrasanta 1971) Journalist and writer. Started at the newspaper *L'Intesa liberale* in Vicenza. At *Corriere della Sera* from 1914 onwards. Sent to Australia and New Zealand in 1925. Dismissed when the Albertini brothers were ousted and rehired by Balzan. Film critic from 1929 to 1941. When Mussolini fell, became director pro tem of *Corriere della Sera* after 26 July 1943. Wanted by the Fascists after 8 September, so fled to Switzerland and stayed in Locarno. After the war, director of *La lettura*, *Il Corriere di Milano* and then *Il Corriere Lombardo*. From 1948 to 1958, editorialist and special envoy for *La Stampa*. From 1952 to 1972, wrote the film column for *L'Epoca*. Author of historical and social pulbications.

SARTORI, ARNALDO (b. Lodi 1888 – d. Milano 1956) Journalist. Secretary to the editor. Works for *Il Guerin Meschino* in 1913 and *La Sera*. News editor, commentator on union issues. Took part in WWI. Entered *Corriere della Sera* in 1925 as secretary general to the administration, and left in 1943. Returned in May 1945 as director of the children's publication *Corriere dei Piccoli*, and then from 1952 to 1955 of the series *I Romanzi del Corriere*.

SIMONI, RENATO (b. Verona 1875 – d. Milan 1952) Journalist and comedy writer. Worked for *L'Arena* of Verona, then after 1899 for *Il Tempo* in Milano. Between 1902 and 1910 author of comedies written in the Venetian dialect. Published satiric reviews and opera librettos for Umberto Giordano. After 1914, theatre critic for *Corriere della Sera*. During WWI, founded and directed *La Tradotta*, newspaper for soldiers of the III Armata forces in the trenches. Worked for *Il Mondo Artistico* and *Il Guerin Meschino* for thirty years, and after 1921 for *Corriere dei Piccoli*.

SOAVI, CLAUDIO (b. Monticelli d'Ongina 1891 – d. Milan, 1967) Private administrator to the Crespi family. Managing director and attorney of *Corriere della Sera* from 1935 to 1938, sent away for "racial reasons." In the autumn of 1943 expatriated to Switzerland, and returned to Milan in the summer of 1945. Managing director of *Il Tempo*.

TAMARO, ATTILIO (b. Trieste 1884 – d. Rome 1956) Journalist, historiographer, diplomat. Student at Innsbruck, irredentist, among the supporters of the Italian University of Trieste in 1905-06 and among the founders of the nationalist newspaper *Idea Nazionale*. Volunteer in the Italian armed forces in the First World War and correspondent for the paper *Il Popolo d'Italia* from 1922. A diplomat from 1927, consul general in Hamburg, Helsinki and Vienna, minister plenipotentiary in Berne from June 1935 to June 1943. Forced into retirement by Mussolini. After the war he published books on Italy during the Fascist regime and the Italian Social Republic.

TORELLI VIOLLIER, EUGENIO (b. Naples 1842 – d. Milan 1900) Journalist. Son of a Bourbon official and a French woman, began his career in journalism after Garibaldi entered Naples under Alexandre Dumas, who was director of *L'Indipendente*. Went on to become director of *L'Illustrazione Universale*. Worked for *Il Secolo* and *Il Corriere di Milano*. On 5 March 1876, founded *Il Corriere della Sera*, which he left after the uprisings of May 1898.

TOSCANINI, ARTURO (b. Parma 1867 – d. Riverdale (USA) 1957) Orchestra conductor. After his diploma in cello and composition at the Conservatory of Parma in 1885, went to Brasil as cellist in 1886 and started a career as orchestra conductor. At the Scala in Milano in 1898, and the Metropolitan in New York in 1908. Artistic director at the Scala in 1920, then permanent director of the Philharmonic of New York in 1928. Resided in the United States from 1931 until 1946. Permanent director of the orchestra of the National Broadcasting Corporation. After the war, returned to Italy to direct the inaugural concert at the Scala after its reconstruction.

TURATI, AUGUSTO (b. Parma 1888 – d. Rome 1955) Journalist and party official. Radical interventionist. Volunteer in WWI. Enrolled in the Fascist National Party (PNF) in 1920 and member of the Fascist squads. Provincial party secretary in Brescia from 1923 to 1926. Member of Parliament from 1924 to 1934, and secretary of the PNF from 1926 to 1930. Lieutenant General of the Militia in 1928. Director of *La Stampa* from 1931 to 1932. Suspended from the party in 1932, then expelled and readmitted in 1937 upon return from exile in Rodi. Did not support the Italian Social Republic (RSI).

VERGANI, ORIO (b. Milan 1898 – d. Milan 1960) Journalist and writer. Started the literary supplement for *Il Messaggero*. In 1926 entered *Corriere della Sera* with travel stories, literary criticism, political invesitgaions, feature stories on cultural life, war correspondence, the cinema and art criticism. Famous for his sports coverage of Europe's most prestigious cycling races, the Giro d'Italia and the Tour de France. After the war, became theatre critic for *Il Corriere d'Informazione* and art critic for *L'Illustrazione Italiana*.

ZANDONAI, RICCARDO (b. Sacco di Rovereto 1883 – d. Pesaro 1944) Composer. Studied at the musical lyceum of Pesaro with Pietro Mascagni. Launched by the publisher Giulio Ricordi, and debuted with *Il Grillo del focolare* in 1908. Among his most successful works, *Francesca da Rimini* (1914) by D'Annunzio, and *I Cavalieri di Ekebù* (1925).